Rogers Park Golf Course
18 Holes of History

By

Lionel Ballard
& Ersula K Odom

Celebrating Rogers Park Golf Course's History, Legends & Families
*Sula Too Publishing * Tampa, Florida*

ISBN: 979-8-9865280-0-7
January 2023 - Sula Too Publishing
www.sulatoo.com/publishing

Printed in the United States of America
Photos and documents are from the archives of Lionel Ballard and Ersula K Odom unless otherwise noted
Florida Sentinel News photos printed with permission from Kaye Andrews

Dedicated to
G.D. Rogers and his family

Contents

Acknowledgment

Many Thanks to The Rogers Family, The Tampa Sports Authority, City of Tampa Parks and Recreation, Golf Association, Rufus Lewis, Mrs. Black Brown, Albert Smith, Freddie Felder, and the Florida Sentinel News.

Introduction

When I was a kid, weekends were spent at Rogers Park with my family. Those weekends were fun and I looked forward to them because we got to play with other kids within our age ranges. Black people had few areas they could go for recreation, but it didn't stop us from having fun.

The kids would play for hours at the playground while their parents listened to and danced to music at the pavilion. We were fascinated with the men and women playing golf around holes that were built by men from the community.

These men used dirt provided to them from the City of Tampa street projects. They had no heavy equipment, therefore they used wheel barrows, rakes, and garden tools to get the job done. They sometimes used spoons to install the holes on the greens. They had to endure snakes, mosquitoes, bugs and other wildlife, but they were determined to build something they could be proud of. Once people heard about the course, players came from around the state to play.

As I got older, my uncle (M.C. Wilder) took me with him to Rogers Park to caddy and shag balls for a few dollars. In high school at H.W. Blake, I played golf with Captain Charles Hamilton, an excellent golfer who won ten amateur tournaments. I was also a caddy for numerous pro golfers who played in the annual Mid-Winter Golf Tournament.

One morning two tour buses arrived at the park to visit the site. I was asked to talk about the history of the park. At that time, I started researching to find as much history as I could find and save for future generations to enjoy. I hope that this book will help preserve the legacy of Rogers Park Golf Course.

Lionel Ballard

Lionel Ballard   Henry Ballard

9

Rogers Park Timeline

Rogers land served as a community park

9-hole course designed by Willie Black & Group

Expanded to 18 holes

1947 —-1951—-- 1952 —1954 —1964

Work began

GD Rogers died

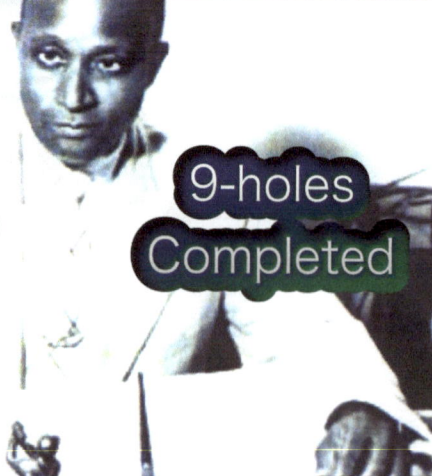

9-holes Completed

Old Clubhouse built

Renovated Course
5 lake added

7/12/2008
National Black Golf
Hall Of Fame

National Registry
Historic Places

Urban Golf Club
Began

New
Club House
Built

1966-1976-1977-1991-2002-2008-2014

TSA Began
Management

11/12/2014
National Registry
of Historic Places

First Tee Began

ROGERS PARK
GOLF COURSE
RONALD M. GARL GOLF COURSE ARCHITECT
LAKELAND FLORIDA

Benefactor and Namesake

DR. GARFIELD DEVOE ROGERS, SR.
(For whom Rogers Park and Roger Park Golf Course were named)

Dr. Garfield Devoe (G.D.) Rogers Sr. was born on January 23, 1885 in Thomaston, Georgia and was an entrepreneur, community leader and philanthropist in Tampa and Bradenton, Florida. He first made a living dipping turpentine in Thomaston but dreamed of greater things. In 1905, he walked along railroad tracks from his home town to Bradenton, Florida selling railroad ties to buy food and passage along the way.

He first opened a dry cleaning and tailoring business on Ninth Street in Manatee County crafting suits for $13.50; it was his first of many profitable businesses. Mr. Rogers owned 5 funeral homes. He also founded Central Life Insurance Company (in Tampa, Florida) that sold insurance to blacks during segregation, and turned into a multi-

million dollar business after he took over as its president in 1933. Mr. Rogers purchased a court house building that was going to be demolished and moved it to land that he also bought which became the first public high school (Lincoln Academy) in Manatee County. He served as Lincoln Academy's first principal in 1930. G.D. Rogers bought the building shown (a former courthouse in Manatee County). He had it moved to Palmetto where he donated it to become the first high school building for blacks in the county.

With the help of Thurgood Marshall, Chief Legal Counsel for the National Association for the Advancement of Colored People (NAACP), he campaigned to get equal pay for black school teachers in the 1940's. His daughter, Louise Johnson became the first black member of the Manatee County School Board.

(Rogers photo courtesy of HCPLS)

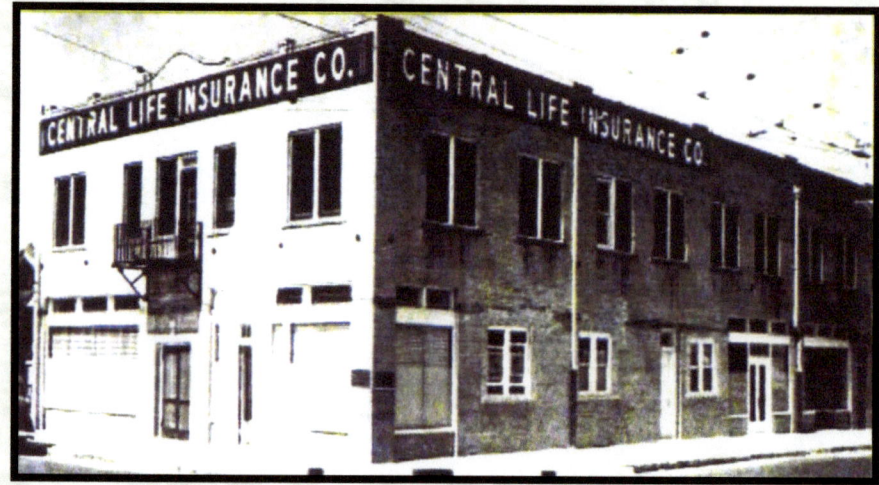

Central Life Insurance Company (Courtesy HCPLS)

Aside from Central Life Insurance Company, Mr. Rogers was an owner and major investor in Rogers Hotel in Tampa, where blacks would stay at a time of overt racism in America.

He also invested in Bonnet Lake Lodge, a lake property with cabins, horses, a lake beach and boats. He also invested in Atlantic Oceanfront property that later became know a Bethune Volusia Beach near Daytona, Florida and the Dolphin Motel on the beach

Lincoln Academy was the first public school in Manatee County for black students. (Photo: Manatee County Historical Archives)

in Jekyll Island, Georgia. Bethune-Volusia Beach, U.S. A1A, 6 miles south of New Smyrna Beach. Educator Mary McLeod Bethune, insurance executive G. D. Rogers of Tampa, rancher Lawrence Silas of Kissimmee and other black investors purchased this oceanfront property in the 1940s to develop a black residential resort community and recreation area.

He was a philanthropist who also owned land on the Hillsborough River in Tampa, Florida not far from his Tampa residence, and donated this property to the City of Tampa to serve as a public park for blacks. At a time when blacks could not enjoy recreation with families and friends at public parks with whites.

Mr. Rogers and his wife Minnie L. Rogers had 16 children but seven died from complications.

While they had a home in Bradenton, their main family home was in Tampa. During this time blacks (Willie Black and others) who caddied for white golfers at Palma Ceia Country Club and who loved the game, could not play with whites, but wanted to play. Mr. Black and other local golfers asked for permission and were allowed to landscape and build a 9-hole golf course at Rogers Park. Later an additional 9 holes were added and Rogers Park then became an 18-hole (par 72) PGA styled public golf course and the site of play for black golfers including Lee Elder, Charlie Sifford, Calvin Pete, Jim Dent and many others.

Prior to the golf course being built, Rogers Park had been solely used by the local African-American community in Tampa for picnics, baseball games, and general recreation activities often after church on Sundays.

G.D. Rogers, Sr. died in 1951. The procession for his funeral stretched over 50 miles. Several State of Florida officials and Congressional Representatives were in attendance; many of the attendees stood outside of the church which was later named in his honor as Rogers Memorial United Methodist Church.

Some members of the G.D. and Minnie L. Rogers's family still reside in Tampa and Bradenton, FL and continue to collaborate and partner with the black community, among others to preserve and protect the history and legacy of Rogers Park and Golf course. In recent years, the Rogers Family formed an ad-hoc committee, "Citizens Who Support Keeping Rogers Park Public". This community engagement was facilitated by the Tampa Organization of Black Affairs in a successful negotiation that led to significant improvements that included renovating the original clubhouse, pavilion, building an adjacent clubhouse building, some course re-design and construction, re-sodding, new water sprinkler system, allowing the 1st Tee program to train disadvantaged youth how to play golf via an on-site program.

The Rogers family and the black community with the support of the black media (The Florida Sentinel Bulletin, WTMP 1150AM, The

Rogers Memorial United Methodist Church

G.D. Rogers Garden Elementary School

Florida Courier), various civic and community organizations and leaders along with members of the Rogers Park Golf Club processed applications and provided testimony to and received assistance and support from the City of Tampa Mayor, City Council Members and City of Tampa Architectural Review & Historic Preservation; State of Florida, Bureau of Historic Preservation and U.S. Government National Park Service officials to successfully register and preserve Rogers Park Golf Course as an official National Historic place.

The National Register of Historic Places is the official list of the Nation's historic places worthy of preservation. Authorized by the National Historic Preservation Act of 1966, the National Park Service's National Register of Historic Places is part of a national program to coordinate and support public and private efforts to identify, evaluate, and protect America's historic and archaeological resources.

It is totally appropriate that Rogers Park Golf Course is named after African American businessman and philanthropist, Garfield Devoe (G.D.) Rogers, Sr., who donated the land for a park and golf course to serve the African American community in Tampa. The original portion of Rogers Park that became a golf course is now listed in the National Register of Historic Places at the local level under Criterion A in the areas of Black Ethnic History, Social History, and Entertainment/Recreation. The original 9-hole golf course was designed by Willie Black, an African American caddie who worked at the private, segregated Palma Ceia Golf Course in South Tampa. He constructed the course with the help of volunteers, some of whom were also golf caddies. Work began on the course in 1947, and Rogers Park Golf Course opened in 1952, with Black as the head golf professional. There were six other amenities of the original park that included the golf course constructed for the use of African Americans along with a tennis court, a baseball diamond, a mini-golf course, a playground, and a picnic pavilion. In 1954, the course was expanded to 18 holes when an additional 9 holes that were constructed on an adjacent parcel of property to the west.

During the era of segregation Rogers Park and Golf Course attracted African American golfers and families who also enjoyed the recreational facilities. The course attracted black golfers from all over the country and many other African American sports and entertainment celebrities. After the golf course was desegregated in 1963, it became a golfing destination for amateur and professional golfers throughout the nation. [1]

(The above information was provided by James Ransom, grandson of the G.D. Rogers, Sr. on behalf of the Rogers Family)[2]

Rogers Park-Early Memories

It Was A Family Affair

The Smith Brothers' Rogers Park Story

Collectively the Smith Brother's stories have become a major part of Rogers Park's history, especially for preserving the spirit of the early days.

Albert Remembers:

Top of mind for Albert was the televised program shown on the Golf Channel highlighting Municipal Golf Courses, "munis" narrated by Junior Walker who Albert caddied for as a teenager. Walker was only 21 years old when he first visited Rogers Park and he was a skillful player. He was nicknamed the Drummer because all he did was play golf every day, or as often as he could. During that time, he lived in New York and later relocated to California.

The Smith Brothers: Eddie, Herbert, Albert, Samuel, Aaron and David all fell in-love with the game at a very young age. Stanley, the baby brother, was considerably younger and didn't catch the 'golf fever'.

We represented a small minority of African Americans in Tampa, or anywhere else, who dared to venture into uncharted waters of playing golf. We were young and unencumbered by the basic societal stigma and limitations of playing golf.

As with everything else during those times, life challenges were an everyday occurrence. We could see the racial divide. As a family, our parents, particularly, our father, wrapped a protective blanket around his children; and that was for his girls and his boys. We played other sports, but mostly unorganized and most often in field spaces around our home. Any interest we expressed in playing organized regular community-based sports like basketball, football or baseball would be short-circuited by our father. He redirected us to find a job, even if that meant working with him on his part-time jobs at night.

Our introduction to golf and making money as caddies satisfied an expectation for us help with school expenses and any little household needs we could assist with. However, as young boys, Rogers Park was our freedom to do with what we chose. As a group, Daddy allowed us to follow Eddie (we called him 'Junior'). Essentially, he was our baby-sitter-Herbert may have been 12 or 13; I was 11 or 12. While Junior always protected us, he was oftentimes, worst than Daddy; but we obeyed him, because that was the way we were raised. The real deal was we didn't want to be left behind!

Albert Smith

Through his high school years, Junior became 'the man' in Rogers Park golf. He, along with Charles and Amos Hamilton, Albert Bell, and Johnny McKinney, among others, represented the new wave for young golfers at Rogers Park. The younger Smiths, Herbert, Albert, Samuel, Aaron, and David all stayed with the game over the years; and respecting David's passing in 2012, we, with life-years behind us, are as engaged as we ever were.

During Junior's prominence, golf scholarships were like a whisper in the African America Community in Tampa. The mumbles of likely possibilities didn't catch on-even Junior couldn't grasp the possibility of playing golf at the college level. We are still amazed at the legacy of golf Florida A&M University nurtured. I lettered in golf from 1965 through 1969; and for six years, Herbert, Samuel, Aaron, and David also dominated their conference competitions in occupying the four top seeds in FAMU Golf. The legacy was sealed in 2002 when Herbert was inducted into the FAMU Hall of Fame of Golf.

During our teen years, most of the guys our age were not interested in golf. While caddying introduced us to golf, the real props were the local players themselves; Willie Black, MC Wilder, Walter Rainey, Tom Brown, Ed Henry, Joe Waiters, Hebert Dixon, PY, Johnny Isaac, Poly, Mr. Clark, Sergeant, Dr. Bunch, Dr. Jackson, Dr. Hewitt, Dr. Andrews, Reverend Willis...We caddied for these guys; they were great, but they represented a job to us-and they taught us the game! These are just some of the names at Rogers during the 'nine holes' era.

Tournament play had a regular cycle which meant touring the nine holes twice to get an eighteen holes score. This was an era where caddies either had pull-carts or carry-the-bag. The bigger caddies often carried doubles.

Golf carts revolutionized the game when you consider golf as a business; and businesses have always and will continue to promote change to increase profitability. Golf, as a business changed a long-standing norm in golf. During the initial period of professional golf, caddies were primarily African American. As the sport took on a more public spotlight, and as it became more commercial, the culture of caddies changed. White caddies replaced the black caddy as the new normal in the golf workforce; and thus, caddies can make millions, not only from caddying but from commercial endorsements as well. This vicious cycle repeats itself in every aspect of American society.

An equal highlight in our teen years was when the Mid-Winter Golf Classic came to Tampa. African American golfers, both professional and amateurs, from all over America came to compete. While everything about this tournament was African American, white golfers also came and competed; and the host welcomed their participation. Of course, they were well known among those black golfers who toured for a living. For us caddies, we were in our glory. We tagged on to a favorite player and repeated that cycle year after year. Jimmy Taylor, Herman Dubois, and Eldorado Long were the primary drivers for starting and promoting this tournament over the years. Their efforts were coordinated with

Eddie Smith

Willie Black, Head Professional, and architect of the first nine holes.

Reflections from Eddie:
Guys in the neighborhood, Jimmy Jackson, George Myrick, Johnny McKenny, and Albert Bell, all lived in the projects. We went to the same school and I used to run track. They were all taller than me, but the stamina was not there for them. I used to beat them. So they asked me one day, if I wanted to go with them to make some money caddying. I didn't know anything about caddying or golfing. I told them I said I don't know; I have to go ask my mother and father, which I did. They agreed that I could go, as long as I did not get into trouble.

I started going to the park with them. We walked all the way from 22nd and Lake. The only things out there were orange groves, woods, and the county hospital, which was the only building along the way. Nothing but woods all the way to the river. The city dump was right across the street, on the left side, all but the parking lot. The nine holes golf course was not completed. There were only a few holes finished but they were still working on the rest of it with shovels and whatever other available equipment; and guys came out and help.

Every one of those guys on the plaque at No. 10, I knew every one of them. I mean they were great guys. "Back in those days it was more about the mens game, where the men would be the players". There were some ladies too; maybe 5 or 6. They were way up in age- Dr. Andrews receptionist, Ms. Tess, used to play. Then caddies and pull carts were all you heard about. Mr. Montgomery's daughter used to play. But another family that used to come out was the Hamilton's. There were 4 or 5 of them. Charles and Amos, Gene and Norman would join in too. These were just some of the early families.

Rogers Park was a family recreation atmosphere; and it was separate and distinct from the golf course. The Park was the site for weekend family gatherings. Family outings were in abundance. Every weekend, families would gather in this carnival-like atmosphere for barbecue cookouts, play, music, dancing and to enjoy friends and neighbors away from home.

The park was an amusement park with golf played around it. There was also a baseball diamond where Luther Rogers used to play baseball, and a tennis court. They would have tennis tournaments supported by Dr. Andrews and Kelly Best. That is how I started liking tennis by working the tournaments as the ball boy.

The baseball diamond was where hole 13 is at now. The city would arrive on Monday, Wednesday and Friday and clean the ground including the baseball diamond, the tennis courts, Ferris wheels, the swings and the putt-putt golf course. The putt-putt course was named Dr. Braggs Miniature Golf which was where hole 16 sits now."

The park was a public facility, so Tampa had to take care of it. We didn't think about how that public facility was maintained that much because we were kids. But when you think about the concept you know

David and Sammie Smith

Albert and Eddie Smith

21

Tampa, the county or the city had to take care of it. The city dump was there. Monday, Wednesday and Friday they arrived with 4-6 lawn mowers and long bed dump trucks. They dumped all the garbage cans and got the big pitch fork and cleaned the whole place up, every Monday, Wednesday and Friday.

All of this had to be done because the park was the only place black Americans could come. People from West Tampa came here too. It had to be maintained. It was a city facility and this is where we gravitate to socialize and be with friends. Polk County, every body, this was the only place they could come. Even people from Clearwater, St. Pete", everybody. You name it, they came to Rogers.

A long time ago when schools were getting out, classes held parties. All the black schools and neighborhoods used Rogers. Yellow school buses arrived at Rogers with the kids from black schools to hold their closing-for-the-summer parties. Again, this was the only place blacks could go.

"Like I said, those were some pretty high times back then with all the families and friends". You met some of everybody. It was more fun then. Rogers Park is a history that should be maintained. We don't want that to disappear not one iota. We understand that in the interest of history, we were part of a generation that got into golf, and that seems to have been a time when a number of people got into golf, as a club.

We want more young men and women, girls and boys exposed to the game without sacrificing what we love about this facility, without sacrificing what we love and have always known about this facility.

I started in the 1940s. Of the 12 of us children, all of the boys came this way for golf. Families came this way for recreational. We caddied. We had a juke box. We never stopped. We could not play golf at the park until Monday. So, we carved out a little path down in the woods and hit balls into the trees that was the hole. We got so involved in that we would rather do that than caddy sometimes. Mr. Black got mad when he could not find a caddy because we were hitting balls into the woods. Mr. Black was a city employee. He lived in Seffner for a while and then he moved off Chelsea and 39th in a house near to the park. His son Frank used to come out here. He was in the military, and he had married one of the Guzman girls.

The place was packed every weekend. Every weekend it was wall to wall people. Often it was so crowded, they had to rope off the golf course so people would get in the way of people playing golf. The way we hit the ball, the cars would be in the way because people were parking all over the place. People were at Rogers every weekend barbecuing and dancing in the pavilion. The man had to come to the park 4-5 times because there were so many quarters being put in the juke box.

It did not bother golfers that they had to pass by the music and dancing, in fact they enjoyed it as much as the people in the pavilion". Those were the good times.

At one time there was a tournament, The Mid Winter Open, was played at Rogers was a part of the regular UGA circuit. Four guys, Jimmy Taylor, Long, Wyatt, and Herman Dubois, pooled their money to make it happen when Jimmy Taylor returned home in 1956. He is from here and had attended high school in Tampa. His mother, Ms. Shaw, lived on 10th. I got to know her well and she called her son "SON". One day I had been over to the dump and was walking back when I saw a guy standing up on the tee. It was an elevated tee and it was Jimmy Taylor. From that point on they pooled their money and then they added that Mid Winter open in the equation.

Teddy Rose won the first tournament. Lee played in this tournament also. Lee was there but Teddy won the debut. It was still 9 holes and they went around twice to make it 18. Who was caddying for Doobie when he was in the running? He played off with Lee Elder.

It was exciting. We were all young teenagers. These guys came to town, put on a big tournament in February where people came from all over the United States. We were hoping to caddy for Jimmy Taylor's wife who came to get us from Middleton after school every

day and took us to caddy. We developed that relationship and we would come in every day to caddy. Man you could make $50.00 in three days. That was a lot of money. They were spending a lot of money and that is what we did. They gave us clubs, they gave us balls and we caddied. This tournament was part of the Senior Tour, where they played in a different city every week. Lee Elder, Teddy Rhodes, Althea Gibson, Willie Brown, James Black, and Jackie Robinson played at Rogers. If you name a name they played in the Mid-Winter tournament.

When we made $5.00 or more, our parents wanted to meet these people to see whether we were lying about the money we made. Our parents didn't play. They wanted to know where we got this money from. We didn't have a problem because we were working for it. We knew what would happen if we lied. We invited some of the guys to our parents' house-our Mom cooked and we had a great time. We developed and maintained a very good relationship.

When players like Jackie Robinson participated in the tournament, the crowds were large and it was really tough". It also wasn't a black thing. Jackie had white, black, blue and green in his crowd trying to get autographs. "Everybody came out".

The other black guy that was the first black in the American League, Larry Doby. Every year Doby came here, he got with me and we became friends. My son and grandson are proud of the pictures they took with Larry Doby. We went to Red Lobster with his wife, and daughter. I carried him to Ybor City because he wanted to know where I got my cigars from. Every year he came, he looked me up.
.

Due to segregation, some black famous people could go anywhere and some could not. Joe Louis is probably the only one who could go anywhere he wanted to go during that time. Don Newcomb "Big Don", a pitcher for the Dodgers could not. Big Don came through here when he was getting ready to go play in China or somewhere not in the United States. The entertainers who could not, gravitated to Rogers and Tampa. We got a chance to see every one of them. They all used to stay out at Clatch Lights. And yes, they used to party. What she did every year was just turn the hotel over to them.

As for the tournaments themselves, we had some very good ones. One was the play off between Lee Elder and James Black. Another was the play off with Herman Dubois and Lee Elder. You know who was very strong during that era, Charlie Owens and his brothers. The Owens boys of Winter Haven came here and they were very strong. Very strong, very good golfers. They always had a good match.

The history of Rogers Park is unique because it was such a magnet for so many people of color that from all the surrounding counties, Pinellas County, Polk County, and Hillsborough. Also, there were quite a few whites who came to the park and were accepted. In fact, Dick Mass also won this tournament. He was at Florida State and used to hang out in the-late 60s and early 70s. He remembered us from back in Tallahassee during our college days.

Another white guy, Marty Pergel, was on the tour. He played the regular tour back in his day. However, this was the only place where we could play each other. We certainly had a number of white golfers come here and they participated. Golf is just that way. First, we did not say you can't play here; well we couldn't say it, but we wouldn't say it. That is just what golf is except in that "other" world.

When they came through here they played with Willie Black and with everybody else. They played with my brother. They developed a very strong game and then they wanted a better club in Tampa. They put him up to play against white, black, blue, and green guys. White kids, from houses across from what is now 22nd, used to come over and play with us. They were playing golf. Their names are long since forgotten. We would not tell them "no you can't." They came over and we had fun.

It was a nurturing place for all young people to be able to come and learn the game of golf. Some white people talk about growing up at Rogers Park by coming in by bicycle, by walking in with their bags and playing here for 50 cents a day. They could play all day and get home by dark by heading home when the sun went down.

During the 60's River Grove area was all white and black kids walked to Rogers from Belmont Heights and Jackson Heights after school. There were some struggles at times and walking through the neighborhood became fearful. Even though my brother did not back down from anybody, walking through the neighborhood sometimes young guys got into battles. Then it became a racial thing. Often we walked from Middleton. We would walk anywhere to get to play. Sometimes we even had to fight Doberman Pinchers. We really had problems with them, but I was not afraid of them. We were determined.

During high school, I would set my schedule where I had a PE class and a study period for the last two periods, and I would ask coach if it was okay to leave to go to the golf course. He would always say yes, go ahead. Coaches organized a golf team at Middleton and nobody knew how to coach it.

Very few blacks played golf and certainly couldn't coach it. I am the one that taught Coach Abe Brown how to play and he liked it. Then, he got to loving it. Another person was Charles Kennedy. He wanted to play and that is how we formed a golf team. In fact, we never lost a match.

The park changed and lost families when they had the ability and opportunity to go other places. That was a loss for the community but to us it was nothing but an expansion of golf to 18 holes for us. We were young men about the time this happened. We were concentrating on trying to play golf. This was a good thing for us. It opened it up for the larger capacity. More and more it became integrated. Sometimes it seems like Rogers have more white players coming through than black players. It is a good facility and it is centrally located. So the expansion to 18 holes was nothing but an expansion of golf to us. [34]

Mary E. James also remembers Rogers Park as a family and community destination. "I, Mary E James, am the granddaughter of Ada T. Payne and a retired Hillsborough County school teacher. I remember my days as a Girl Scout "Brownie" from around ages 8 to 12. My Girl Scout leader was Mrs. Thomas who I remember as "pristine and proper". Mrs. Thomas expected a lot from me, beginning at the YWCA on Kaye Street and Central Avenue. Once a week we sold Girl Scout cookies and during the summer we had a two-week Girl Scout camp at Rogers Park. While there, we learned to make a stove by cutting a hole in a 10 pound can and using Sterno flames for heat. We cooked and ate hamburgers and hotdogs. Everything was homemade.

I remember such activities at Rogers Park as plant giveaways, including Christmas trees at Christmas, and family outings. At the park, we played on the merry-go-round, sliding board, and swings. I still smell the fresh scent of pine trees, as well as the fallen pinecones that we collected and decorated for Christmas.

There was a snack stand where we bought pickled pig feet, cookies, chips, and other snacks. I don't recall cooked food, even though there may have been. Rogers Park was a popular place to go for our family my fond memories linger.[5]

Little **Mary Elizabeth Morris (James)** found family fun at Rogers Park and she brought joy to countless young people as a lifetime educator and champion for Booker T Washington Elementary School and all it's students. Shown here is Ada T. Payne(her grandmother whose portrait hangs in Robert W Saunders Library), little Mary, and adult Mary E. James.

Tees: Lionel Ballard recalled that trees played a key role in determining where people wanted to park their cars and camp out for the day. Shade was priceless and highly sought after.

Girl Scouts (Courtesy of James Ransom)

Ethel, Lee & Bettye Davis (Courtesy of Bettye Davis)

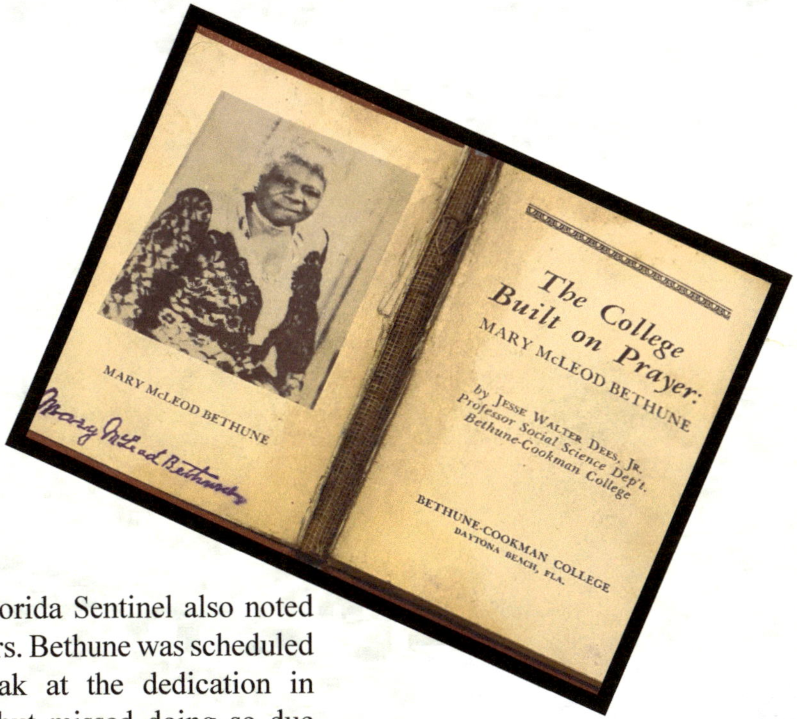

The Florida Sentinel also noted that Mrs. Bethune was scheduled to speak at the dedication in 1952, but missed doing so due to a traffic delay.

Bettye Davis' memory of Rogers Park documents the presence of several local and national legends. She remembers being assigned the task of presenting roses to Mary McLeod Bethune following her speech at the park. Bettye was five years old or younger and terrified. Mr. & Mrs Lee Davis, however, made sure their young daughter was on stage with them for this historic occasion. Through her tears, Bettye gave two dozen roses to the lengendary Mrs. Bethune. Bettye was rewarded for her courage, by Mrs Bethune, with a signed copy of her childsized biography.[6]

As a young teacher, **Doris Ross Reddick** who became the first black woman to chair the Hillsborough County School Board, shared that she took her students to Rogers Park as often as she could as a reward.

The park was family social favorite. The place to go for young people to see their friends, as these teenage girls.

Perry Harvey Sr & Lee Davis, second & third from left respectively. (Courtesy of Bettye Davis)

Dr. Kermit Harvey, Perry Harvey Sr.'s grandson, fondly spoke of caddying for his grandfather at the park.

Perry Harvey, Sr, for whom the Perry Harvey Sr. Park is named, led the dockworkers union 1410 for 30 years. His son, Perry Harvey, Jr., became the first black Hillsborough County Commissioner.

Lee Davis, a wealthy black multi-business owner for whom The Lee Davis Center is named, donated property to establish a health clinic for Tampa's black community .

Harold Watson "Charlie Ragg", Louis "Police", C. B. Andrews "Paper man", "Andre White", Earl L. Monroe "Mighty Mite", Billy Brown "Hustler" (Courtesy Rufus Lewis)

Original buildings

(Courtesy of Ersula K Odom)

The Evolution of Rogers Park Golf Course

The First Men's Golf Association at Roger Park Golf Course 1952

Front row from L-R: Eston Sheppard, Raymond Patterson, Leander McGriff, Gus Brant, Alexander Broom, Thomas Mention, Homer Hemingway, Lovetter Hemingway, unkn, Herman Curtis, Jerry Mann, and Kentucky.

Back row from L-R: Unkn, Luther Wright, unkn, Hector Mero, Leo Griffin, unkn, Clarence Hamilton, Edward Montgomery, unkn Slim, Willie Black, unkn, unkn.

Not shown: M.C. Wilder, Tom Brown, Elmer "Red Shirt" Smith, Joseph Waters, Buddy McClain, Raymond Dixie, Johnny Issac, P.Y. Dipper Dan, James Taylor, Herman Dubose, Hommy C, Ed Henry, W.O. Bunch, Carl Dixon, Leroy Lewis, Sr. Rev. John Willis, Rev. Francis Davis, Rev. Charles Kennedy, Robert Nunnerly, Bill Lewis, Pro James Black, Richard Lewis, Herbert Dixon, Charles Hamilton

Ladies: Mary Black, Gwen Tucker, Freddie Wilder, Tess Murray

TAMPA GOLF CLUB MEMBERS: Louis H. Carter, Archie Mond, Richard London, Arthur Smith, Gainous Byron, Bob Moore, John Kinsey, Freddie Starling, Herbert Fisher, Equilla Davis, Wayne Brookins, Charlie White, Rufus Lewis, Robert Sutton, James Young, Randolph Smith, Charlie Tolliver, Bennie Milford, Leonard Campbell, Ted Brown, Willie Black, Arlanders Alford. (Courtesy Rufus Lewis)

Early Women Golfers
At Roger Park Golf Course

Mrs. Gwen "Honey" Tucker was the first black woman to play golf at the newly constructed Rogers Park Golf Course. In a news article appearing the the Florida Sentinel Bulletin on February 6, 2009, she recalled her experence. Tucker learned to play with a driver and and 2 iron given to her by caddies from Palma Ceia Golf Course. She often watched them play near Dobyville school.

She recalled playing on a long stretch of land and just hitting balls. Since it was too expensive to purchase clubs, she played with the two she was given. They also had to hit around kids because Rogers was used a baseball diamond as well. It was a Sunday playground. Families would attend church, go home to change clothes and then head to the park.

Though reluctant at first, women began to play, organized and even had a tourament where the prize was a turkey. Mrs Clara Davis was the president of the women's organization.

The names she recalled were Buddy and Mae Yeoman, Mrs. Essie Mae Rainey and her husband, M.C. Wilder, Joe Waters, O. C. Collins, Terria Jones (of St. Petersburg), and Mrs. Okeretha Montogomery (Mrs. Edmund Montgomery - a former caddie).[7]

Shown here are several women who played golf at the newly created Rogers Park Golf Course in the 1950s. Some of those shown are : Ms. Ophelia Hopkins, Ms. Evelyna Gillespie, Ms. Evelyn Black, Ms. Irene Scarborough, Ms. Gwen "Honey" Tucker, Ms. Essie Mae Rainey, and M Clara Davis. Mrs. Tucker was the first black woman to play golf at the newly constructed Rogers Park Golf Course. (Courtesy Rufus Lewis)

Present layout

The Original Nine Hole Layout

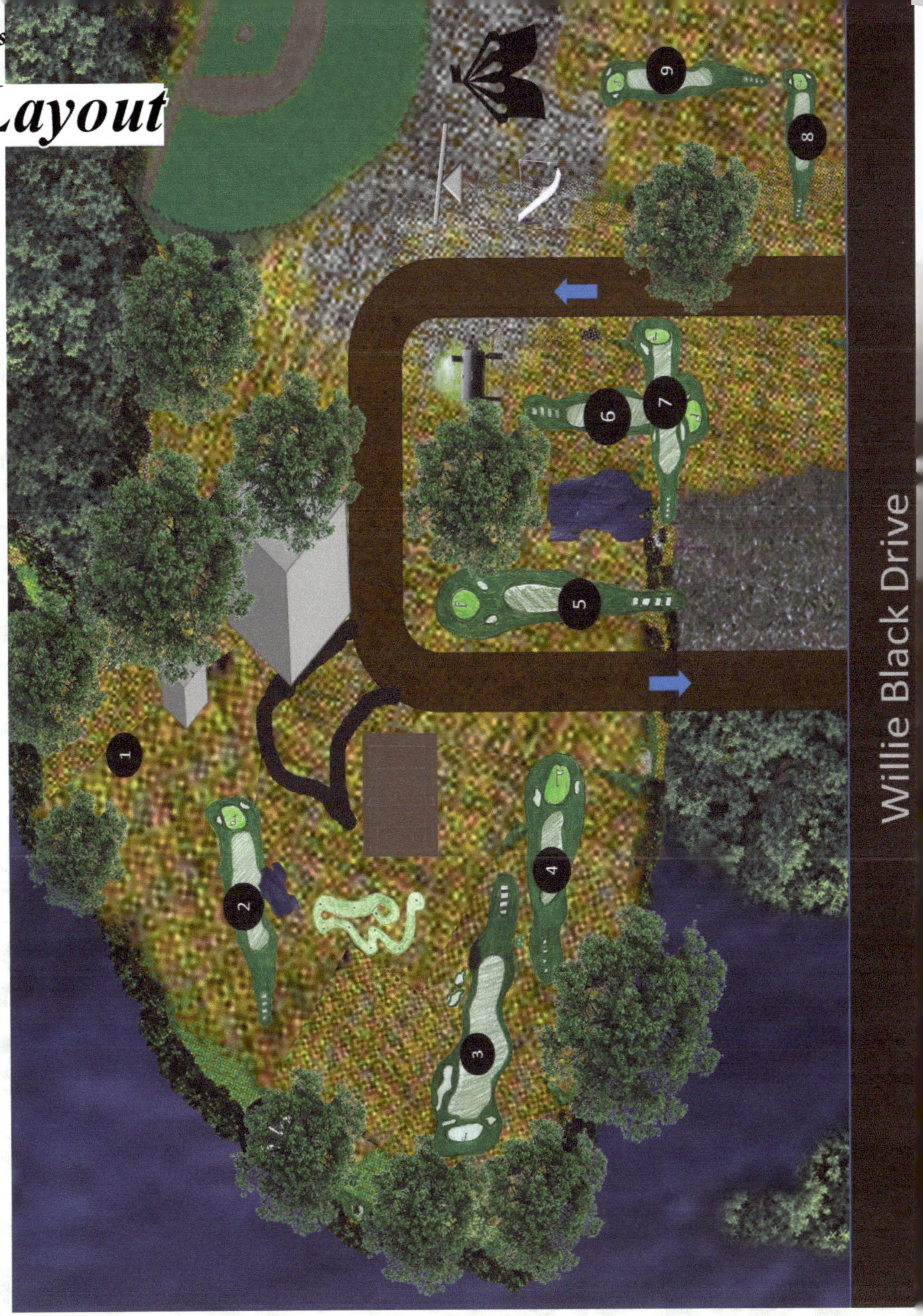

Hole 1 Par 4
Hole 2 Par 4
Hole 3 Par 5
Hole 4 Par 5
Hole 5 Par 3
Hole 6 Par 4
Hole 7 Par 4
Hole 8 Par 3
Hole 9 Par 4

Willie Black Drive

The Original Club House

Golf Course Renovation

"Golfers Prayer: May the good Lord grant - fore golfing days are done
That I might just once score - a- legitimate hole in one." (unknown)

C. Blythe Andrews, Jr., the Andrews Family and Rogers Park

C. Blythe Andrews, Jr., his father, C. Blythe Andrews, Sr. and his brother, Dr. W.W. 'Billy' Andrews were instrumental in helping what is now Rogers Park Golf Course to become what it is today.

The elder Mr. Andrews was a financial contributor in the early 1950s, when Mr. Willie Black and other black caddies working at Palma Ceia Country Club were grant permission to build a 9-hole golf course.

Mr. Andrews, Jr., and his brother regularly played golf at the course. Mr. Andrews, Jr. was known for his colorful matching golf outfits and even owned his golf cart.

In 1975, Mr. Andrews Jr., became the first black person to serve on the newly formed Tampa Sports Authority. He served as chairman of the Golf Course Committee.

In 1976, the City of Tampa gave management rights to the newly formed Tampa Sports Authority, and under Andrews, a $400,000 renovation project began. Mr. Andrews served on the Sports Authority Board for 8 years and served as the Board Vice Chair, dedicating a lot of his attention to improvements at the beloved Rogers Park Golf Course.

After his term ended, Mr. Andrews, Jr.'s brother, Dr. W. W. Andrews was appointed to the Tampa Sports Authority Board and was instrumental in a $4 million renovation at Rogers. The irrigation system was replaced, and the greens were completely rebuilt. In 2001, a new maintenance compound was completed followed by a new clubhouse in 2002.[8]

C. Blythe Andrews in golf gear.
(Courtesy Kaye Andrews)

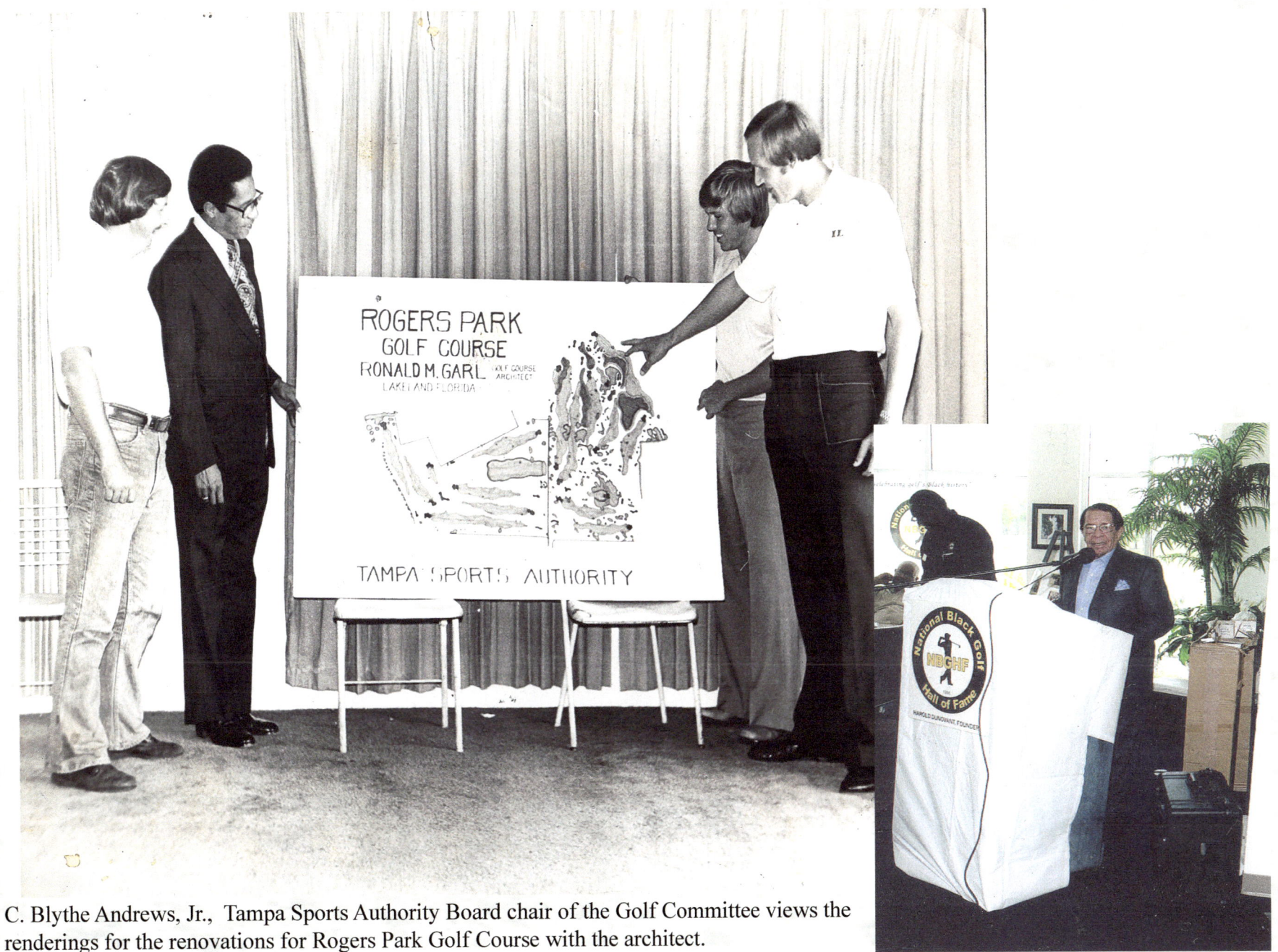

C. Blythe Andrews, Jr., Tampa Sports Authority Board chair of the Golf Committee views the renderings for the renovations for Rogers Park Golf Course with the architect.
(Courtesy Kaye Andrews)

C. Blythe Andrews, Jr.
Inducted into Black Golfers Hall of Fame

At ground breaking ceremony for park renovations with Mayor Billy Poe

Standing in front: Alton White, Mayor Billy Poe, and Harold Watson

Original Rogers Park site certificate currently hangs in the Pro Shop and is available to the public

Pro Charley Owens is shown on the left observing new driving range balls being hit by Dr. W. W. Andrews, while Harry Nesbitt also looks on. (Courtesy of The Florida Sentinel News)

Pro Charley Owens is shown receiving two engraved pictures from the Rogers Park Golf Association to be hung in Rogers Park Clubhouse. Pictures are of Mr. G. D. Rogers, for whom the Rogers Park is named, and of Mr. Owens' signing day as a professional. At right is Bobby Scott, a member of Rogers Golf Association. (Courtesy of The Florida Sentinel News)

Golf Course Dedication

Minnie Rogers, G.D. Rogers' widow, is receiving a plaque in honor of G.D. Rogers during dedication of the newly renovated park. (Courtesy of The Florida Sentinel News)

Alton M. White, left, executive assistant to Tampa Mayor Bill Poe, is receiving a plaque from Rogers Park Golf Association for steering the renovation of the Rogers Park Golf Course. Presented by C. Blythe Andrews Jr.(Courtesy of The Florida Sentinel News)

Legendary
Head Professionals

In order of their service:
1 Willie Black
2 Charlie Owens
3 Harry Morrow
4 Michael Cooper
5 Kennie Sims
6 Larry Bruner
7 Bill Gainer
8 Vince Reid
9 TJ Heidel

1 *Willie Black*

JOHN BUCKHART   WILLIE BLACK

(Courtesy Rufus Lewis)

Willie Black was born December 26, 1914 in Albany Georgia and graduated from Albany State College with a Agriculture degree. As a child, "The Pro", worked around an uncle who was a greens keeper at a golf course. It was here that Willie Black's love for the game developed. By 11 years old, he was at constant practice in the back woods where he lived. By age 16, he had developed a golf game that was so concise and exact that his reputation spread around the United States.

He worked as a chauffeur, hired in Cleveland, Ohio, then moved to Florida and worked on the rail road. He left the railroad and worked at Rogers Park and as a caddy at Palm Ceia Golf Course.

He started getting involved in polities at election time. He helped get blacks to vote and transported those who needed a ride to the polls. During a candidate's sponsored fish fry and campaign for voters, one candidate running for mayor was asked if he would promote a golf course for blacks at Rogers Park, he agreed and when he won, he kept his promise.

Black and Mr. Hector built the first three holes using tin cans and spoons. Nine holes were built by hand. There were so many golfers coming to Tampa, the City said they would have to charge a fee. Tickets were issued to each golfer and Black bought golf carts.

An article was written about the course and golfers from all over came to see and play at Rogers Park. Pro baseball players in Tampa for spring training were among them.

Then a large club house was built and the additional nine holes by hand. Charlie Sifford, Lee Elder pros and Eddie Smith helped create the greens.

Professional Champion In
Mid-Winter Open Golf

Charles Owens of Winter Haven holds the Seagram's Seven Crown trophy as the winning professional in the Seventh Annual Mid-Winter Open Golf Tournament played at the Rogers Park Golf Course last weekend. Looking on is Nathaniel Starks of Atlanta and St. Petersburg, who lost sudden death playoff to Owens on second hole after Owens, Starks and George Wallace had all posted one under par 141's. Both Owens and Starks hold PGA Touring pro cards.

(Courtesy of The Florida Sentinel News)

2 Charlie Owens

Tuesday, March 4, 1969.   Fla. Sentinel Bulletin-Published every Tues. & F

Charles Owens Wins Mid - Winter Open Golf In Sudden Death Playoff

Charles Owens, a handsome 6 ft. 3 inch long knocker from Winter Haven, has what the experts would call two major handicaps in golf. He walks with a pronounced limp caused by an auto accident several years ago and he belts the ball cross-handed.

But Owens, always smiling always concentrating when necessary as he exchanged pleasantries with the huge gallery following him, came through with a par on the second hole of sudden death playoff to win the Seventh Annual Mid-Winter Open Golf Tournament at Rogers Park from Nathaniel Starks and George (Potato Pie) Wallace, both of Atlanta.

Owens apparently had the tournament sewed up coming into the 17th hole one stroke ahead of Starks and Wallace and all three lying two only inches from the Par 5 hole. Starks putted up four feet from the hole, and Wallace chipped up about three feet past. Then Owens unaccountably blooped his chip shot straight up in the air to his left, away from the green, but putted up and sank it for what he thought was a par 5. Starks and Wallace two putted for fives. At the 18th tee, Owens was told he got a 6 because he had hit his ball twice on the bloop shot.

"It was my word against their's," Owens later said on the 18th green. "But I guess that's golf. I'm still going to win." After all three men parred the 18th and Carl Seldon of Atlanta blew his chance for a four way tie by missing a two foot putt on the 18th ten minutes later, Owens promptly went out and won. The victory was good for $400. Starks and Wallace earned $245 each, while Seldon, former SIAC champion made $175.

Larry Youngblood of Chicago won in the championship flight among the amateurs with a 152. Thomas Mathis, Green Cove Springs, was second at 153, and the defending champion, Dr. W. W. Andrews defeated former Blake High star Charles L. Hamilton for the third trophy on the first hole of sudden death playoff. Both men finished at 154 for 36 holes.

James Pierce, Jacksonville, won in the First flight with a 159, while Alonzo Perry, former baseball star and Harlem Globetrotter, was two strokes back at 161. R. Stephens won the third trophy with a 162.

O. James Gilchrist of Tampa beat Sylvester Denmark of Winter Haven for first place in the Second flight. Both men had 169's. O. Collins, the first round leader, faltered to a 172 which was good enough for the third place trophy.

H. Spence won first place in the Third flight with a 189, while J. Wright took second at 193 and J. Cunningham was third at 194.

Prof. Edward J. Henry of Clearwater, playing excellent golf all the way, fired a 159 to easily win first place among the Seniors. J. Littleton and Charles (Lefty) Baldwin, both also from Clearwater, were tied for second at 166, with Littleton winning in sudden death playoff. The favorite, Coach James Everett of Miami finished fourth at 167.

Gertrude Styles won among the ladies with a 193, while Maxine Meares shot 195 and Mrs. S. G. Black 286 for the third trophy.

Black Receives Award

Two special awards were made after play Sunday. Charles Owens was the recipient of the Seagram's Seven Crown trophy as the pro winner. Willie Black, pro at Rogers Park since 1951, received a cash award from Dr. Robert D. Greene, Columbus, Ga., as "Pro of the Year." Dr. Greene told the Sentinel Bulletin Black was selected by the Public Relations Council of Golf which embraces Illinois, Florida, Georgia, Missouri, Alabama and Oklahoma. The award was made possible by Budweiser, Seagram's Seven Crown and First Flight Golf Co.

"Because of his outstanding and unselfish administration of the Rogers Park Golf Course, Mr. Black was presented this award," Greene said. He added that the award will become an annual affair.

PROFESSIONALS

Charles Owens, Winter Haven, $400, 141; Nathaniel Starks, St. Petersburg, $245, 141; George Wallace, Atlanta, $245, 141; Carl Seldon, Atlanta, $175, 142; James Walker Jr., Los Angeles, Calif., $140, 142; Joe Lee Mathis, $103.33, 144; Charles Hill, $103.33, 144; Thomas Brisbon, $103.33, 144; Curtis Sifford, $80, 145; Howard Brown, $80, 145; Freddie Carter, $80, 145; Tommie Walker, $80, 145; Elrado Long, $75, 148; Willie Jefferson, $50, 149; Bobby Strobde, $50, 149; Robt. Lee Walker, $50, 149; D. Pearce, $50, 149; George Johnson, $50, 149; Eugene Clapp, 150; Alfred Blair, 150; Noah W. Heeder, 151; Walker Lee Moore, 151; Kenneth Sharp, 152; Isaac Small, 153; Reginald Golden, 153; Jimmy Clark, 153; Zeke Hartsfield, 153; Harvey Hayes, 154; Jimmy McMillian, 154; Walter Kerchenski, 154; Bran Matus, 155; John W. Bell, 157; James Brantley, 157; Willie Demps, 157; Luther Johnson, 157; E. Williams, 158; Harold "Round Man" Dunovant, 158; Willie Dillard Jr., 161; Charles Stepps, 161.

PROS WHO WITHDREW

Pete Jones 82, E. Williams 79, B. Shell 80, George Butler 81, H. Middleton 82, S. Thompson 82, T. Cupinacci 80, M. C. Wilder 83, Fred Owens 80, Marshall Bradley 80, Sam Duncan no card, T. Williams 79, Ray Parles 82, George Mims 82, F. T. Rivers 81, Frank Stephens, 111 81, Donable Bisbee 94, Preston Knowles 83, Charles Bennett 81, Carl L. Brown 89, Ike Pinckney 79, Eddie Smith 93, Frank Boyd 85, E. Carmichael 96.

CHAMPIONSHIP FLIGHT

Larry Youngblood, Chicago, 152; Thomas F. Mathis, Green Cove Springs, 153; Dr. W. W. Andrews, Tampa, 154; Charles L. Hamilton 154, Doc Reeves 157, W. Cassidy 157, Charles Brown 158, B. T. Harris 169, M. Stewart 160, J. Jones 161, H. Franklin 161, A. House 162, Clyde Gray 162, Charles Kennedy 163, Elmer Smith 167, R. Whisby 168, Larry Crandall 83 withdrew, R. Seldon 81 withdrew, W. Vinson 74 N C.

FIRST FLIGHT

James Pierce, Jacksonville, 159; Alonzo Perry, Chicago, 161; R. Stephens 162, Ernest Hayes N.C. 92, F. Wright N.C. 93.

THIRD FLIGHT

H. Spence 189, J. Wright 193, J. Cunningham 194, E. Francis 197, R. Floyd 200, H. Hergzo 201, E. Collins 207, W. F. Black, Jr. 210, T. Robinson 259.

SENIORS

Edward Henry 159, J. Littlejohn* (won playoff) 166, Charles Baldwin 166, James Everett 167, H. Stoffer 169, L. Fisher 173, B. Brown 178, S. L. Hall 179, B. Hill 179, Dr. R. W. Greene 211.

LADIES

Gertrude Styles 193, Maxine Meares 195, S. G. Black 286, 163, A. Longmire 165, Dr. W. O. Bunch 166, J. Walker 168, E. Branburn 169, Harold Watson 170, R. Smith 172, R. Founderburk 173, W. B. Meyer 173, A. Tiroc 174, T. Jenkins 177, J. Smith N.C. 84, B. Brown, N.C. 84, B. T. Hayes withdrew 84, B. Gay withdrew 84, J. McClinton withdrew 85.

SECOND FLIGHT

O. J. Gilchrist 169, Sylvester Denmark 169, O. Collins 172, A. Smith 173, C. B. Andrews, Jr. 174, McCoy Pigee 174, J. Washington 174, G. Sowell 177, J. Smith 177, H. Rutledge 178, W. H. Ross 178, J. Warren 181, A. Hamilton 183, H. Williams 185, R. Morgan 186, B. Jackson N.C. 88, C. Youg N.C. 89, T. Crawford 92.

(Courtesy of The Florida Sentinel News)

3 Harry Morrow

Very little is known about Harry Morrow, however, we know that he was head pro at multiple golf courses including Rogers Park. The document to the right shows him as head professional and manager of Rogers Park

Golf is a humbling game

Even when you bust a big one straight down the middle . . .
Even when birdies come your way

ROGERS PARK GOLF COURSE
234-1911

* Championship 18 holes
* Pro Shop
* Snack Bar
* Lounge
* Driving Range
* Lessons
* Golf Clinics

7910 N. 30th Street
Tampa, Florida 33610

Harry Morrow
Head Professional/Manager

MARGARET'S RESTAURANT

"COME ONE COME ALL"
TRY OUR HOME COOKED MEALS

1724 N. Nebraska Avenue
Tampa, Florida 33605

APACHE ANSWERING SERVICE, INC.

WE CARE

1715 Tampa Street
Tampa, Florida 33602

GENE & ORIS BARBON   229-1913

Phone: 251-9502

NAT AND CAROL'S HAIR DEN

featuring
THE BEST IN HAIR CARE and STYLES

Open Daily 10 am. to 7:00 p.m.
Closed Sunday's
1707 N. Howard Ave   Tampa, Florida

WISHING TAMPA GOLF CLUB

MUCH "SUCCESS"

WITH THEIR 2ND ANNUAL

PRO-AM GOLF TOURNAMENT

Francis Davis & Family

Rogers Park Golf Course advertisement in the Willie Black PRO-AM Golf Tournament booklet

4 Michael Cooper

Reflections

So what was the significance of the Mid Winter Golf Classic weekend? First, re-enacting the event rekindled fond memories for many of the local residents. The Mid Winter event was once a mainstay on the old United Golf Association (UGA) tour, a series of golf tournaments showcasing the talents of African American golfers. Our records indicate that the first Mid Winter Open occurred circa 1962, at Rogers Park Golf Course, in Tampa, FL. The founder of the event was Jimmy Taylor, who lived in New York, but was originally from Tampa. JT, as I came to know him, competed on the circuit. More importantly, he successfully hustled money and used it to stake aspiring pro golfers. He convinced his closest comrades to put forth dollars to create a fun and meaningful weekend in Tampa. Among those joining his efforts were Herman DuBois, Eldorado Long, and Harold Wyatt; all legends in the folklore of black golf.

Truth be told, it was people who hustled and made money like Jimmy Taylor that made pro events for African American golfers a reality. Others included Sam Sims in Nashville, Moses Stevens in Los Angeles, Blood, Saginaw Pete, and Square Washington in Chicago. There are more, and others with a deeper sense of history than me can present other significant names from the past. I, for one, think this part of our history should receive more attention, be documented, and remembered.

Back to the Mid Winter. We were able to retrieve old newspaper clippings/articles from Dr. William Andrews, a local Tampa dentist. Doc Andrews is the brother of C. Blythe Andrews, owner of the Florida Sentinel Bulletin. The newspaper caters to the African American and inner city community, and has served this niche market for 87 years. Both Andrews' brothers were pioneers, and instrumental in creating and preserving the legacy of Rogers Park. They both served as board members for the Tampa Sports Authority and City of Tampa, and often challenged the political regimes to do the right thing as it pertained to Rogers and the community at-large. C. Blythe Andrews died in January 2010, just days after we announced the re-creation of the Mid Winter Golf Classic weekend. He will be remembered for his contributions to Rogers

Park and Tampa, and we know he would have been proud of our weekend. Doc Andrews provided pictures and stories from former Mid Winter Open' s from 1968- 1972. Winners were Bobby Stroble, who competed in this year's version, Howard "Lefty" Brown, James Black, and Charlie Owens. A review of the past participants is literally a who's-who in black golf. The names and stories bring a smile, as well as a source of pride. It meant a lot to me to play a role in bringing this event back to our community.

Next was the inaugural Advocates Pro Tour event, the name given to the professional competition within the Mid-Winter weekend of activities. Our event in Tampa launched a proposed series of pro events designed to identify and assist African American golfer's advancement to the PGA Tour level. The concept is to do so by providing them a place to compete and sharpen their skills, ala the old UGA. At the end of the series, one deserving player will receive full sponsorship into the 2010 PGA Tour qualifying tournament. The Advocates USA group is a nonprofit organization, comprised of approximately 80 African American businessmen. Each has had success in their respective business endeavors, is an avid golfer, and advocate for change. This group is very different from prior sponsors with similar intent. In fact, I have never before witnessed a group come forward with the collective resources and singular purpose as this one. With just a little outside support, they could rapidly help promote the plight of African American golf in competitive play (and business). It's exciting to be a part of this group!

Everyone is aware of the lack of African American competitors on the PGA and LPGA Tour's, for the obvious void is displayed on television each week. But what about business? The business aspect needs to become a more intentional focus for people of color, in my opinion, a topic that was discussed at our Friday night symposium. Let's review a few statistics. First, though, let me preface this by pointing out that when talking to organizations within the golf industry, it is typical for the information to get more· difficult to retrieve, as the questions pertaining to ethnicity and gender get more specific. Why? My guess is that it is either because agencies are not tracking demographics, or

because they are guarding against being singled out for a lack of diversity. I speak from experience on this, as I recently had a special assignment to help gather comparative data across the industry related to diverse participation rates, competitive play, employment, and supplier diversity. Below is a brief, but relevant, sample of recent data. More is available.

In a recent industry study commissioned by the World Golf Foundation, it was reported that golf generated a total economic impact of $195 billion, creating approximately 2 million jobs with wage income of $61 billion. In a separate study, a 2009 report gathered data from 50 golf related organizations. From a sample size of 5,000 employees, only 8% were African American. Further, in more anecdotal conversations between folks like you and I, less than a dozen names of African American individuals could be identified in leadership roles within the golf industry. Less than a dozen individuals in a $195 billion industry, with over 2 million jobs? Why so few?

The National Golf Foundation annually produces a detailed report on total rounds played. Their reports indicate that total rounds played have been on a gradual, yet continuous, decline each year since 2005. The blame, they stated, was due to poor weather and a weak economy, to which few would argue. One might also argue, however, that these declines are due, in some part, to the demographics amongst golfers remaining unchanged since 2003. Let me explain ...

Over the past decade the face of America has shifted in terms of people of color and gender. America is now a country with a 34% minority population, and 52% female. Both of these numbers are predicted to escalate in the next 10-15 years. Some experts forecast people of color will rise to over 40% by 2020, and that females will continue to outlive their male counterparts, thus increasing that percentile, too.

Meanwhile, demographics within the golf industry have remained at less than 15% participation from minority populations (7% for African Americans), and less than 25% from females. In other words, the majority of participants in the game of golf remain Caucasian men, and stagnant (at best), while the face of America continues to become more ethnically diverse, and female. Can golf survive without changing the demographics?

From a business perspective, where are all the African American golf professionals, teachers, merchandise reps, grounds superintendents, and CEO's? Where are the golf course architects, journalists, manufacturers, and club designers? As a race, why are we so absent/invisible in the golf industry? And what must be done to get more people of color involved? These are important matters that require immediate attention, with a high degree of intentionality. We've waited long enough for passive and/or incidental efforts to work. They haven't.

There was some momentum created at our symposium as many ideas relative to employment and business, competitive play, and education surfaced. It is important that we continue this dialogue. I will forever

remember the beginning portion of the evening, when people were being introduced. I could not help but marvel at the abundance of talent assembled under the same roof. Think of what could be accomplished by utilizing this amazing talent towards a common cause. I will also always remember the importance of positive role modeling, mentoring, and leadership provided by Don Wright, as he told the story of Adrian Stills and the click, clack of spikes on the cart path. Tremendous story, and testimony to the fact that we need people of color in prominent

leadership positions as examples to our younger generation.

Still, I also could not help but wonder how talented must one be to get an opportunity to excel in this industry? At what point is one deemed smart enough, experienced enough, talented enough, professional enough? Surely there were many in that room that could help the game and the industry become more welcoming and inclusive. Why have so few been asked or put in positions to help?

Perhaps we should become more proactive ourselves and begin to create meaningful strategies to increase inclusion. Then, we could encourage the golf industry to demonstrate more interest in promoting these strategies. It's worked in other sports, and certainly worked in corporate America. Were you aware that NASCAR has a formal diversity initiative? So does hockey, soccer, and tennis. NASCAR, hockey, soccer, and tennis, but not golf. Really! Does it make sense that golf can continue to be so non-diverse, but have no formal plan to address diverse matters?

Another special highlight from the Mid-Winter weekend was the National Black Golf Hall of Fame dinner and induction ceremony. The recognition given to Winston Lakes GC, Barbara Douglas, and John Merchant were deserved, and the speeches were eloquently delivered and heartfelt. The crowd was special, too, and it was remarkable to have had former Tour players like James Black, Jim Dent, Bobby Stroble, Adrian Stills, Jim Thorpe, and Tom Woodard under the same roof. Rarely happens. Couple that with notables like Derrick Brooks, Rhonda Glenn, from the USGA, Earnie Ellison from the PGA, Pete McDaniel, author of Uneven Lies and formerly with Golf Digest, and you have something really spectacular. This is the sort of attention and celebration worthy of our Hall of Fame. We need to all work together to make the next one even more visible and memorable. It's that important!

Several things have happened since our March weekend. At the symposium, Marilyn Hubbard informed the group about a project in Detroit involving their collection of municipal golf courses. We learned that a Request for Proposal was out, and the City was seeking a management company to assume controls of four golf locations. She informed us that they had assembled a local group to specifically identify a minority-controlled management group to match the high percentage of African American population in Detroit. At the symposium we learned that two African American management companies currently exist. One, SydMar Golf Management, is owned by Marie Jackson Donovant, who participated in our weekend. She is also the wife of Jeff Donovant, Executive Director for the National Black Golf Hall of Fame, and son of its founder, Harold Donovant. It's believed that both management companies will bid on the Detroit muni operations. Best of luck, and let's hope for the best.

Other potential developments include getting more participants to academy type lesson environments for specialized training. This concept was discussed at the symposium. We hope to continue these discussions and create solutions in this area. Shortly after our weekend, I participated in a conference call where a few facilities were mentioned as possible locations. Among those were the PGA Learning Center in Port St Lucie, FL. Another was Innisbrook Resort, owned by Dr. Sheila Johnson. Personally, I believe those are two dynamic possibilities, as long as our African American professionals are included.

There are other potential locations. I know that Adrian Stills is currently involved in a construction project to renovate the teaching area in Pensacola, FL. Tom Woodard has access to multiple operations in Denver, CO. Kennie Sims is already planning academy features at Rogers Park in Tampa, and Craig Bowen recently accepted a pro teaching assignment with the TOUR Academy Learning Center, at World Golf Village in St Augustine, FL. Let's continue to explore all of these possibilities.

Just as important are the conversations surrounding historical preservations. We briefly learned about the collaboration between the PGA and USGA to collect and display artifacts from African American golfers. I am sure we will hear more as that continues to develop. You might recall that John Merchant spoke of one Hall of Fame in his acceptance speech in Tampa; similar to Major League Baseball. There have been follow-up conversations with the appropriate parties for further discussions. More to follow on that, too.

I'd like to mention that there are a couple of other things worthy of preservation and longevity. One is Clearview Golf Club, the first course built and owned by an African American family (the Powell's). Another is the Bill Dickey scholarship association. I am sure there are others. My point is that we should rally to commemorate and preserve the handful of places/things that have been so instrumental in the history of golf and our culture. The generations behind us deserve that!

Finally, there is one last thing deserving mention. An African American female golfer named Alice Brown competed in the Tampa event as a professional. A week or so prior to the event she was told that she could compete, but would have to do so from the same tee boxes as the men. Undeterred, she never complained, posted her score for the 36-hole event, and was a gracious competitor throughout. As I thanked her for participating, I couldn't help but to ask why. She told me her purpose was to bring attention to the lack of opportunities for African American female professionals. I believe her efforts were bold and courageous. I also believe in her cause, for she is absolutely correct. I will remain in communications with Alice, and assure everyone that we will do all possible to address the concerns of female players, too, as we continue this journey for inclusion.

Kennie Sims, Mike Cooper, Bob Arnot, Harry Morrow

5 Kennie Sims

KENNIE SIMS, MBA, PGA

For over three decades, Kennie Sims continues to be among the most visible proponents of development and inspiration in the golf industry. Currently, Kennie is the Vice President of Golf Operations for the Tampa Sports Authority. His primary duties include managing a staff of 200 people, coordinating and supervising daily operations, long term and strategic planning for three City of Tampa owned golf courses: Babe Zaharias Golf Course , Rogers Park Golf Course, Rocky Point Golf Course. In addition to his daily duties in 2017, Kennie successfully took over the management of the Hillsborough County owned Fairway Cafe. As a result, he has successfully managed a $4 million operating budget and a combined $5 million in capital improvements. In 2015, Kennie served as the project manager for the $1 million Rocky Point Golf Course renovation. Furthermore, Kennie's tireless dedication to his industry has resulted in servicing over 1 million golfers and visitors over the past ten years. Kennie also volunteers his time to community based programs and to the PGA of America.

As a PGA professional, Kennie is always seeking ways to be in front of trends and initiatives for the North Florida PGA (NFPGA) Section and the PGA on a national level. In 2018, President Suzy Whaley reappointed Kennie to the PGA of America Membership Committee. The Membership Committee focuses on preserving the PGA Constitution and Bylaws and evaluates the standards of PGA membership. In addition to serving on the PGA of America Membership Committee, Kennie serves as the Diversity and Inclusion Chairman for the NFPGA. As the Chairman, Kennie is responsible for regularly identifying leaders, providing education, and tracking progress. In 2016, Kennie was asked to serve on the NFPGA Foundation, which is responsible for developing and maintaining fundraising strategies designed to support local charities. Since 2017, Kennie has served on the NFPGA Finance Committee, which is empowered to provide financial oversight of section affairs.

Kennie continues to represent the golf industry by serving on the World Golf Foundation - We Are Golf Diversity Task Force whose mission is to promote and increase diversity and inclusion across the game and business of golf. Kennie works with PGA HOPE (Helping Our Patriots Everywhere) at Terrace Hill Golf Center, a program that empowers wounded veterans through golf. Since 1991, Kennie has been a charter board member of The First Tee of Tampa Bay. TFITB impacts junior golf in Tampa by providing golf and life skill programs by reinforcing values like integrity, respect and perseverance. Kennie volunteers his time to Derrick Brooks Charities. The mission of this charity is to provide educational opportunities for socio-economically challenged youth. Kennie is a board member of No Strings Attached (NOSA), a nonprofit designed to supply essential services and clothes to the homeless population of Tampa.

Kennie earned his MBA at the University of South Florida and completed his Business Administration undergraduate studies at Fayetteville State University (NC). He was been awarded Golf Professional of the Year twice by his peers in the PGA of America, he has served as President of his chapter of the PGA.

Kennie resides in Tampa, Florida and has two children, Kevin and Leslie. He is a savvy executive that enjoys sports, backgammon, travel and personal growth.[9]

#5 Kennie Sims, #1 Willie Black, #4 Dr. Cooper, #3 Harry Marrow

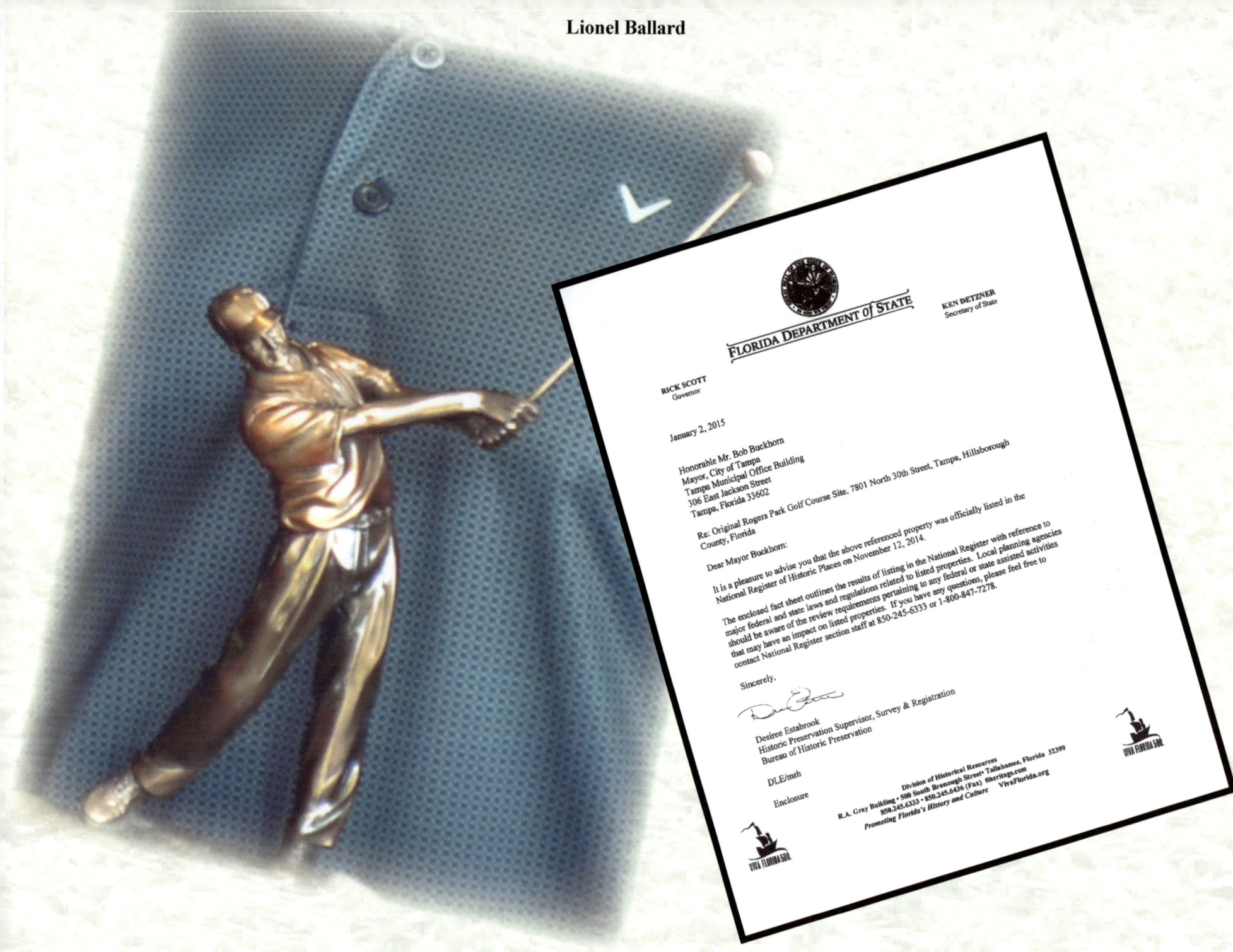

L arry Brunner worked at Roger Park from August 1980 until March 1981 and went to the Hall of Fame golf course for two years. He returned to Rogers Park on February 14, 1983 and was there until November 1998. He played in a bunch of North Florida Pro-Am's and West Florida pro and Plus 40 Tournaments. He played on the National Senior Tour which started in 2000. Qualified for and played in Florida Senior Tour tournaments, the Florida Senior Tour Open in Naples, finishing second twice. [10]

6 Larry Brunner

7 Bill Gainer

Bill was born and raised in Tampa and educated in the Hillsborough County school system. In 1966 at age 17, he was recruited by the IBM corporation to be a part of a program to develop inner city kids to work at Kennedy Spacecenter. After eight months of electronic training, they were assigned to different departments based on exhibited skills. With his high mechanical aptitude, he was placed in mechanical department with the understanding if it didn't work he would be reassigned. It worked out very well. He worked about 1.5 years before being drafted in army. He served 3 years in the Army Signal Corp, attaining rank of Sargeant (e5).

This is when and where he began playing golf. Upon completion he returned to IBM at the spacecenter in 1971. In January 1974, Gainer was accepted into IBM's Large Systems Division in Orlando, Florida where he worked until 1986 - the year his mother died. He requested a hardship transfer to Tampa to be near his father and worked primarily in St Petersburg and the Dunnedin areas until 1996. He retired after working 30 years.

After being a member at Roger's Park for a while, Gainer began working parttime in the cart barn. After a few months Larry Brunner asked him to be his assistant and he accepted in December 1996. Gainer became Head Pro around 2003 and remained until his retirement in 2007. He moved to Columbia, Alabama and served on the Town Council and as Assistant Mayor. He has two children who live in Orlando, Florida and one in Wyoming.[11]

8 Vince Reid

Vince Reid was born in Gastonia, North Carolina in August 1954, raised in Greensboro North Carolina. He graduated June 1972 from Greenboro's J.B. Dudley High School where he played on the golf team and participated in several other sports. Reid received a golf scholarship to attend Fayetteville State University(FSU) from 1973 – 1977. He started the golf team that competed in the Central Intercollegiate Athletic Association (CIAA) and was elected team captain for four years. He led Fayetteville State University's team to the CIAA Championship title in 1976 and 1977. He was voted CIAA player of the year in 1976 and 77; ALL-CIAA team 1993 – 1997; inducted intto the FSU Hall of Fame; and inducted into the 1992 Fayetteville Athletics Hall of Fame. Reid graduated from Fayetteville State University in May of 1977 with a BS Degree in Business Finance, Marketing and Accounting.

He joined Lake Pontchartrain Golf Course in New Orleans, LA as their Assistant Golf Professional from 1978 to 1980. From 1980 to 1981 he played at Madden Park Golf Course in Dayton Ohio. Reid relocated to Tampa in 1981 to pursue a career as a Professional golfer. He played on several mini tours and attempted numerous qualifiers for US Open and other PGA tournaments.

Reid accepted position as Director of Golf and Junior Golf Program Director at the Chi Chi Rodriguez Foundation in 1992 and held the position until 2000. He started the Vincent Reid Foundation and Academy of Golf, operating from 2000 to 2020 with the goal of making golf accessible to all kids regardless of their economic ability, race or disability.

Vince Reid served as Head Golf Professional at Rogers Park Golf Course from approximately 2007 to 2009. He was appointed Chairman of the Board and Chapter Director for HOPE Worldwide Tampa Bay from 2010 to 2021[12]

9 TJ Heidel

T.J. Heidel is the Director of Golf at Rogers Park Golf Course Operations. He is responsible for the general administration, management, coordination, and supervision of the day-to-day activities. Rogers Park Golf Course plays 30,000 rounds of golf and generates over $800,000 in revenue annually; with a staff of 35 employees and volunteers.

T.J. began his career with the Tampa Sports Authority in 1995. T.J. held positions of Head Golf Professional at Rogers Park and Bebe Zaharias Golf Course before being promoted to Director of Golf at Rogers Park Golf Course in 2013. T.J. has been teaching the game of golf to all ages since 2005. His teaching philosophy is "Keep it simple, because you are never too young or too old to learn this amazing game.

T.J. Completed his B.S. in Human Services and Master of Business Administration at Springfield College. He is a Tampa native and lives locally with his wife Lisa, and their three children. His hobbies are undertaking DIY projects, spending quality time with family and playing golf.[13]

Legendary Tournaments

Buster Aligiano
KAPPA
OMEGA
Tampa Fire Fighters
City of Tampa Black Heritage Committee
Height Classic
FAMU
Tampa Park & Recreation
Middleton High Scholarship
Club YANA
ONYX Ski Club
City Men Amateur
Doug Williams
Mid-Winter Open

Rogers Park Golf Course
6th ANNUAL MID-WINTER OPEN
GOLF TOURNAMENT
February - 22 - 23 - 24 - 25 - 1968
TAMPA, FLORIDA

SOUTHERN
GOLF ASSOCIATION
6th ANNUAL
CENTRAL FLORIDA
MID-WINTER OPEN
GOLF
TOURNAMENT
THE NEW ROGERS PARK
GOLF COURSE — TAMPA, FLA.
FEBRUARY
22ND—23RD—24TH—25TH
1968
(54 HOLES)
4 AMATEUR FLIGHTS — 12 TROPHIES
1 FLIGHT FOR THE LADIES
1 SENIOR FLIGHT
PROS: Play 54 Holes AMATEURS: Play 36 Holes
LADIES : Play 36 Holes

DR. P. A. ERVIN

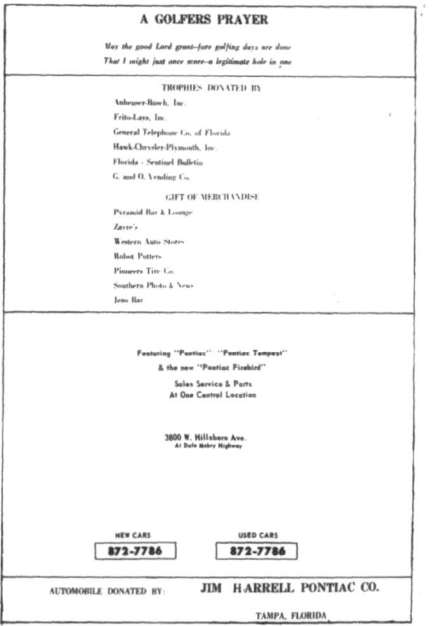

$3,000.00 PRO PRIZES

			70.00	
1st	$600.00	7th	170.00 13th	60.00
2nd	400.00	8th	145.00 14th	50.00
3rd	300.00	9th	120.00 15th	50.00
4th	245.00	10th	100.00 16th	
5th	220.00	11th	90.00 17th	
6th	200.00	12th	80.00 18th	

JIMMIE TAYLOR Tournament Chairman
PROS - $27.00 AMATEURS - $15.00 LADIES -
(Green Fees Included)
PRACTICE ROUND THURSDAY
THE 22nd   In New York
JIMMIE TAYLOR'S GOLF SCHOOL,
              UN. 236-2192
Tampa Area Code 813 - 231-2072
        or
  236-3276...Willie Black

A GOLFERS PRAYER

May the good Lord grant, fore golfing days are done
That I might just once score—a legitimate hole in one

TROPHIES DONATED BY

Anheuser-Busch, Inc.
Frito-Lays, Inc.
General Telephone Co. of Florida
Hawk-Chrysler-Plymouth, Inc.
Florida - Sentinel Bulletin
G. and O. Vending Co.

GIFT OF MERCHANDISE

Pyramid Bar & Lounge
Zayre's
Western Auto Store
Robot Pottery
Pinners Tire Co.
Southern Photo & News
Jens Bar

Featuring "Pontiac" "Pontiac Tempest"
& the new "Pontiac Firebird"
Sales Service & Parts
At One Central Location

3800 W. Hillsboro Ave.
At Dale Mabry Highway

NEW CARS	USED CARS
872-7786	872-7786

AUTOMOBILE DONATED BY: JIM HARRELL PONTIAC CO.
TAMPA, FLORIDA

Tuesday, February 8, 1972   Fla. Sentinel-Bulletin Published every Tues. and Fri.

Bobby Stroble Wins Mid-Winter Open Golf Title And $1,600

Young Bobby Stroble of Albany, Ga., sank an eagle putt on No. 17 in the final round of the Mid-Winter Open Sunday to win first money of $1,600.

Stroble was one over par going into the hole after a bogey on No. 16, when he rifled his second shot to the center of the green and sank a 10-footer for the eagle on the part 5 hole. He calmly parred the final hole in the thirty-

BOBBY STROBLE

Nineteen-Year-Old Star Wins Amateur Title

Bruce Dossett, right, 19-year-old amateur golf star from Greensboro, N. C., won the championship flight of the Tenth Annual Mid-Winter Open Golf Tournament at Rogers Park Sunday with a 36 hole score of 149. Dossett won in sudden death playoff over two other players—Joe Lewis and Jack Towns. Watching Dossett practice putt is Art Gilreath.

six hole affair to edge out Howard (Lefty) Brown of Detroit, and Freddie Carter of Dallas, Texas, by one shot. Stroble finished at one under par 143, while Brown and Carter finished at even par 144. Both Brown and Carter collected $925 each.

Tied for third among the pros were Ron Burnham and James (Junior) Walker at 1 over 145. Each collected $425. Leon Crump and Nate Starks of St. Petersburg they carded two over 146s and pocketed $150 each.

Tournament favorite Charles Owens of Winter Haven was tied with Robert Walker at 147. At 148 were Charles Cross and James Black. All collected $50 each.

Others collecting $50 each and their scores were:

149—Al Green and Ken Sharp. 150—Robert Ford, Ben Perry, William Brooks, Eddie Smith and Bruce Dobbie. 151—Chick Griffith, defending champion Marty Furgol and Joe Wyatt. 152—Mickey Dillard, Carl Seldon, Ron Terry, Clarence Jones and George Wallace. 153—Noah Wheeler and George Butler. 154—Chuck Mason, Robert Owens and Pete Clark.

FREDDIE CARTER

156—Charles Lindsey and Jimmy Clark. 157—Bill Shivers and Jack Beattie. 158—Isaac Small.

Dossett Wins Playoff

Brilliant shotmaker Bruce Dossett, a 19-year-old from Greensboro, N. C., won a sudden death playoff on the first hole with a par to capture the championship flight among the amateurs. Dossett shot a two under 70 Saturday but ballooned to a 79 Sunday and was tied by James Towns and Joe Lewis. Towns fired a 73 on Sunday to close the gap while Lewis had a 76 to go with a 73 on the first day. Those in the flight included Mark Guttenburg, one shot back at 150. Jasper McClinton and Tom Knapp at 151. Coleman (Peanut) White 153. Willie Davis 155. Herbert Smith and Todd Crandall at 156, and Dr. W. W. Andrews 163.

Smith Wins First Flight

Sam Smith of Tampa won the first flight with a 154, with Horace Jackson taking second at 155, and William Vincent of St. Petersburg third at 156.

John Stephens of St. Petersburg won the second flight with a 157. Al James was second at 166, and George McCray, Lincoln Morehead and Calvin Johnson tied at 167.

William H. Ross of Clearwater won the third flight in a playoff with Bob Peddy. Both finished at 179. Third in the flight was Lloyd James.

Mrs. Vera Gillespie won the ladies flight with a 203. Second was Mrs. Gertrude Styles at 210, and third was Mrs. Vera Williams at 234.

The 1972 Pinto auto was not won because a hole-in-one was not scored in the tournament.

Herman DuBois and Jimmy Taylor, New York residents and co-founders of the Mid-Winter Golf Turnament

(Courtesy of The Florida Sentinel News)

Best Players In Amateur Field At Mid-Winter Open

These three happy men won the top trophies in the Championship Flight at the Seventh Annual Mid-Winter Open Golf Tournament played at Rogers Park last weekend. From left: Larry Youngblood, Chicago, first place; Thomas Mathis, Green Cove Springs, second place; and defending champion Dr. W. W. Andrews of Tampa. third place. Youngblood posted 152, Mathis 153 and Dr. Andrews 154. Dr. Andrews won on first hole of sudden death playoff from Charles L. Hamilton, former Blake High golf star. Hamilton also had 154.

(Courtesy of The Florida Sentinel News)

(Courtesy of The Florida Sentinel News)

Top Three Players Among Amateurs In Mid-Winter Open

The top three players among amateurs participating in the eighth annual Mid-Winter Open Golf Tournament at Rogers Park last weekend were from left: John Corbett, Great Barrington, Mass., who finished third; Dr. W. W. Andrews, second place finisher, and Charles L. Hamilton, winner of the flight. Both Dr. Andrews and Hamilton are from Tampa.

(Courtesy of The Florida Sentinel News)

Herbert, Samuel, Aaron, and David Smith (brothers) and team. This was the first of five SIAC FAMU championships. Herbert Smith was number 1 player all four years, and the golf coach after graduation. Herbert was the first player inducted in the Hall of Fame. The Smith brothers were the first brothers, Sam, Aaron, David and Herbert, to play collegiate golf on a team at the same time (1971-1973). They started as caddies at Rogers Park in 1958 starting with Eddie Smith then Herb Smith, Albert Smith David and Aaron (Courtesy of The Florida Sentinel News)[14]

Professional Champion In Mid-Winter Open Golf

Charles Owens of Winter Haven holds the Seagram's Seven Crown trophy as the winning professional in the Seventh Annual Mid-Winter Open Golf Tournament played at the Rogers Park Golf Course last weekend. Looking on is Nathaniel Starks of Atlanta and St. Petersburg, who lost sudden death playoff on second hole after Owens, Starks and George Wallace had all posted one under par 141's. Both Owens and Starks hold PGA Touring pro cards.

Tuesday, March 4, 1969.   Fla. Sentinel Bulletin-Published every Tues. & 1

Charles Owens Wins Mid - Winter Open Golf In Sudden Death Playoff

Charles Owens, a handsome 6 ft. 3 inch long knocker from Winter Haven, has what the experts would call two major handicaps in golf. He walks with a pronounced limp caused by an auto accident several years ago and he belts the ball cross-handed.

But Owens, always smiling always concentrating when necessary as he exchanged pleasantries with the huge gallery following him, came through with a par on the second hole of sudden death playoff to win the Seventh Annual Mid-Winter Open Golf Tournament at Rogers Park from Nathaniel Starks and George (Potato Pie) Wallace, both of Atlanta.

Owens apparently had the tournament sewed up coming into the 17th hole one stroke ahead of Starks and Wallace and all three lying two only inches from the Par 5 hole. Starks putted up four feet from the hole, and Wallace chipped up about three feet past. Then Owens unaccountably blooped his chip shot straight up in the air to his left, away from the green, but putted up and sank it for what he thought was a par 5. Starks and Wallace two putted for fives. At the 18th tee, Owens was told he got a 6 because he had hit his ball twice on the bloop shot.

"It was my word against their's," Owens later said on the 18th green. "But I guess that's golf. I'm still going to win." After all three men parred the 18th and Carl Seldon of Atlanta blew his chance for a four way tie by missing a two foot putt on the 18th ten minutes later, Owens promptly went out and won. The victory was good for $400. Starks and Wallace earned $245 each, while Seldon, former SIAC champion, made $175.

Larry Youngblood of Chicago won in the championship flight among the amateurs with a 152. Thomas Mathis, Green Cove Springs, was second at 153, and the defending champion, Dr. W. W. Andrews defeated former Blake High star Charles L. Hamilton for the third trophy on the first hole of sudden death playoff. Both men finished at 154 for 36 holes.

James Pierce, Jacksonville, won in the First flight with a 159, while Alonzo Perry, former baseball star and Harlem Globetrotter, was two strokes back at 161. R. Stephens won the third trophy with a 162.

O. James Gilchrist of Tampa beat Sylvester Denmark of Winter Haven for first place in the Second flight. Both men had 169's. O. Collins, the first round leader, faltered to a 172 which was good enough for the third place trophy.

H. Spence won first place in the Third flight with a 189, while J. Wright took second at 193 and J. Cunningham was third at 194.

Prof. Edward J. Henry of Clearwater, playing excellent golf all the way, fired a 159 to easily win first place among the Seniors. J. Littleton and Charles (Lefty) Baldwin, both also from Clearwater, were tied for second at 166, with Littleton winning in sudden death playoff. The favorite, Coach James Everett of Miami finished fourth at 167.

Gertrude Styles won among the ladies with a 193, while Maxine Meares shot 195 and Mrs. S. G. Black 286 for the third trophy.

Black Receives Award

Two special awards were made after play Sunday. Charles Owens was the recipient of the Seagram's Seven Crown trophy as the pro winner. Willie Black, pro at Rogers Park since 1951, received a cash award from Dr. Robert D. Greene, Columbus, Ga., as "Pro of the Year." Dr. Greene told the Sentinel Bulletin Black was selected by the Public Relations Council of Golf which embraces Illinois, Florida, Georgia, Missouri, Alabama and Oklahoma. The award was made possible by Budweiser, Seagram's Seven Crown and First Flight Golf Co.

"Because of his outstanding and unselfish administration of the Rogers Park Golf Course, Mr. Black was presented this award," Greene said. He added that the award will become an annual affair.

PROFESSIONALS

Charles Owens, Winter Haven, $400, 141; Nathaniel Starks, St. Petersburg, $245, 141; George Wallace, Atlanta, $245, 141; Carl Seldon, Atlanta, $175, 142; James Walker Jr., Los Angeles, Calif., $140, 143; Joe Lee Mathis, $103.33, 144; Charles Hill, $103.33, 144; Thomas Brisbon, $103.33, 144; Curtis Sifford, $80, 145; Howard Brown, $80, 145; Freddie Carter, $80, 145; Tommie Walker, $80, 145; Elrado Long, $75, 148; Willie Jefferson, $50, 149; Bobby Strobde, $50, 149; Robt. Lee Walker, $50, 149; D. Pearce, $50, 149; George Johnson, $50, 149; Eugene Clapp, 150; Alfred Blair, 150; Noah W. Heeder, 151; Walker Lee Moore, 151; Kenneth Sharp, 152; Isaac Small, 153; Reginald Golden, 153; Jimmy Clark, 153, Zeke Hartsfield, 153; Harvey Hayes, 154; Jimmy McMillian, 154; Walter Kerchenski, 154; Bran Matus, 155; John W. Bell, 157; James Brantley, 157; Willie Demps, 157; Luther Johnson, 157; E. Williams, 158; Harold "Round Man" Dunovant, 158; Willie Dillard Jr., 161; Charles Stepps, 161.

PROS WHO WITHDREW

Pete Jones 82, E. Williams 79, B. Shell 80, George Butler 81, H. Middleton 82, S. Thompson 82, T. Cupinacci 80, M. C. Wilder 83, Fred Owens 80, Marshall Bradley 80, Sam Duncan no card, T. Williams 79, Ray Parles 82, George Mims 82, F. T. Rivers 81, Frank Stephens, III 81, Donable Bisbee 94, Preston Knowles 83, Charles Bennett 81, Carl L. Brown 89, Ike Pinckney 79, Eddie Smith 93, Frank Boyd 85, E. Carmichael 96.

CHAMPIONSHIP FLIGHT

Larry Youngblood, Chicago, 152; Thomas F. Mathis, Green Cove Springs, 153; Dr. W. W. Andrews, Tampa, 154; Charles L. Hamilton 154, Doc Reeves 157, W. Cassidy 157, Charles Brown 158, B. T. Harris 169, M. Stewart 166, J. Jones 161, H. Franklin 161, A. House 162, Clyde Gray 162, Charles Kennedy 163, Elmer Smith 167, R. Whisby 168, Larry Crandall 83 withdrew, R. Seldon 81, withdrew, W. Vinson 74 N.C.

FIRST FLIGHT

James Pierce, Jacksonville, 159; Alonzo Perry, Chicago, 161; R. Stephens 162, Ernest Hayes N.C. 92, J. Wright N.C. 93.

THIRD FLIGHT

H. Spence 189, J. Wright 193, J. Cunningham 194, E. Francis 197, R. Floyd 200, H. Hergzo 201, E. Collins 207, W. F. Black, Jr. 210, T. Robinson 259.

SENIORS

Edward Henry 159, J. Littlejohn* (won playoff) 166, Charles Baldwin 166, James Everett 167, H. Stoffer 169, L. Fisher 173, E. Brown 178, S. L. Hall 179, E. Hill 179, Dr. R. W. Greene 211.

LADIES

Gertrude Styles 193, Maxine Meares 195, S. G. Black 286, 163, A. Longmire 165, Dr. W. O. Bunch 166, J. Walker 168, E. Branburn 169, Harold Watson 170, R. Smith 172, R. Founderburk 173, W. B. Meyer 173, A. Tiroc 174, T. Jenkins 177, J. Smith N.C. 84, B. Brown, N.C. 84, B. T. Hayes withdrew 84, B. Gay withdrew 84, J. McClinton withdrew 85.

SECOND FLIGHT

O. J. Gilchrist 169, Sylvester Denmark 169, O. Collins 172, A. Smith 173, C. B. Andrews, Jr. 174, McCoy Pigee 174, J. Washington 174, G. Sowell 177, J. Smith 177, H. Rutledge 178, W. H. Ross 178, J. Warren 181, G. Knowles 182, A. Hamilton 183, H. Williams 185, R. Morgan 186, B. Jackson N.C. 88, C. Youg N.C. 89, T. Crawford 92.

(Courtesy of The Florida Sentinel News)

ong Huge Crowd At Mid- Winter Open Tournament

widely-known Tampans were among large
rticipating and watching play in the final
the Seventh Annual Mid-Winter Open Golf
ent played at Rogers Park Golf Course
Top photo from left: Harold Watson, Jr.,
Watson, Harold Watson, Sr., Earl Monroe

and Billy G. Mitchell. In bottom photo, Mrs. Eu
Mae Strange, left, and Mrs. Jean Dyson look ov
souvenir program with Jetie B. Wilds, Sr. M
Wilds was co-chairman of souvenir program cq
mittee.

Feb. '69

WILLIE BLACK PRO-AM Golf Tournament

"ROOTS OF GOLF TOURNAMENT"

Pioneer black golfers "returned to their roots" where many of them got thier start in the game of golf. Golfers came from St. Petersburg, Plant City, Lakeland, Sarasota, Clearwater, Sebring, Orlando, Safety Harbor, Gainesville and other areas to participate. Rufus Lewis, tournament director credited the dreams, efforts, and imaginations of the pioneers for many people even getting the to chance to play golf.

During their 17th "Roots of Golf" Tournament some of those recognized were: Willie "Pro" Black, founder, Tom Brown, Ed Henry, Dr. Bunche, Carl Martin, Mike Williams, Morehead and Rainey, Johnson and Fisher, Jones and Oxendine, Thompson and Brinkley, McCray and McCray (father and son), Gainer and Norman, Dewdney and Grady, James and Ramsey, and L. Carter and S. Carter.[15]

Rogers Park Course Record Holders
68 9/28/2001 Gary Koch
68 12/9/2001 Paul Michael
68 1/1/ 2002 Glenn McCall
67 2/10/2002 T.J. Heidel
66 2/10/2002 Lee Carter
64 10/4/2004 Mike Welch
61 1/29/2006 John "Gus" Koskinen
61 1/29/2006 Ron Terry Par 71

City of Tampa Men's Medal Play Championship

1947 Harry Root
1959 Tommy Riherd
1960 Clarence C.C. Martin
1964 Tommy Riherd
1969 Clarence C.C. Martin
1975 Gary Koch
1976 Wayne Rudewicz
1983 Wayne Rudewicz
1984 Wayne Rudewicz
1987 Wayne Rudewicz
1990 Wayne Rudewicz
1991 Justin Trombill
1992 Bill Moore
1995 Don Lucas
1996 Wyatt Meyer
1997 John Fowler
1998 Atsushi Kozaki
 Wayne Rudewicz
2002 Matt Jackson
2003 Matt Jackson
2004 Chase Baldwin
2005 Gary Cona
2006 Chase Baldwin

Rogers Park Rabbit Tour 3-man Team

1998 J. White, J. Adams, and J. Brimmer
1999 G. Valdes, J. Trombley, and J. Alfieri
2000 G. Valdes, J. Trombley, and A. Sadakata
2001 G. Valdes, J. Trombley, and A. Sadakata
2001 L. Brunner, K. Corliss, and R. Caldwell
2002 K. Sims, P. Michael, and M. Fittin
2002 L. Brunner, K Corbliss, and B. Clements
2002 J. Alfieri, J. Wombley, and G. Valdes
2003 D. Welker, J. Assad, and S. Scriver
2004 K. Sims, R. Stormie, H. Smith
2005 Mark Thomas, Mark Weaton, and Matt John
2006 John "Gus" Koskinen, Brad Quirri, and Josh McCumber
2007 Brandon Lee
2008 Noi Clay

Trophy is currently displayed in the club house

Tournaments - Bigger and Better

(Photo courtesy of Freddie Felder)

A Golf Course Design Among The Best

Hole 1: 551 yard par 5, out of bounds on the left and fairway traps on right

Hole 2: 432 yard par4 out bound on left and tree line fairway on right with sand traps in front and back of green

Hole 3: 387 yard par 4 trees on right and sand trap in left front of green

Hole 4: 417 yard par 4 sand traps on both side of fairway and sand bunker on left and right of green

Hole 5: 405 yard 4 with 2 sand traps on right side of fairway and sand bunker on right side of green

Hole 6 154 yard par 3 sand trap in front both side of green

Hole 7: 437 yard par 4 out of bounds on both side of fairway, trees also lines fairway with sand bunker on both side of green

Hole 8: 204 yard par 3 hole bordered by trees , no doglegs or sand traps , and only one water hazard located just beyond the green

Hole 9: 509 yard par 5 hole bordered by only a few trees, but featuring a major waste bunker and a large water hazard

Hole 10: 375 yard par 4 hole has only a slight dogleg and on only one small sand trap located near the green

Hole 11: 371 yard par 4 hole has a relatively straight shot to the green with no major water hazards of sand traps

Hole 12: 202 yard par 3 hole has is a relatively easy hole without traps or other hazards

Hole 13: 399 yard par 4 hole presents a challenge to the golfer , having a strong dogleg, sand traps , and a large water hazard near the green

Hole 14: This 525 yard par 5 hole challenges the golfer with a narrow fairway near the tee, a strong dogleg to the north and two large water hazards midway to the green.

There is also a sand trap just in front of the large raised green

Hole 15: 205 yard par 3 hole presents a narrow fairway with large water hazards on both sides of the fairway , one of which borders the green

Hole 16: 380 yard par 4 hole features a narrow fairway flanked by water hazards just off the tee and a strong dogleg to the southwest. The golfer faces small sand traps before reaching the green

Hole 17: 422 yard par 4 hole has the third longest fairway on the course. This hole also has a narrow fairway and a dogleg. Water and waste bunker flank the fairway , and the terrain rolls just short of the green

Hole 18: 427 yard par four hole is the second longest on the course and has a large water hazard just behind the green

(Photos courtesy of Freddie Felder)

April 30, 2022 was our 7th Annual Golf Tournament which is chaired by Mr. Frank Woodard, a long standing City Of Tampa Black History Committee Inc. (COTBHC) member. The golf tournament is the brain child of Mr. Frank Woodard as a fundraiser for the COTBHC scholarship program. This continuous success of the golf tournament at Rogers Park Golf Course has turned into our major fundraiser for COTBHC Scholarship Fund. COTBHC is in our 24th year of awarding scholarships to our youth in the community. All donations received for our scholarships are from corporate sponsors, community partnerships and City of Tampa employees. Our scholarship program awards scholarships to graduating African American High Schools students in the Hillsborough County School District. The City of Tampa Black History Committee, Inc. is an organization made up of current and retired City of Tampa employees and was started in 1988 under the direction of Mr. Bobby L. Bowden former Director of Community Affairs with the City of Tampa under the leadership of Mayor Sandra Freedman. My name is **Celeste Gibbons-Peoples**, Past President of COTBHC, Katrina House, COTBHC President

City of Tampa Black History Committee 2022 Tournament
Winners: Elena Figueroa, Chuck Wyatt, Tim Carr, Jeff Brown

(Photos courtesy of Freddie Felder)

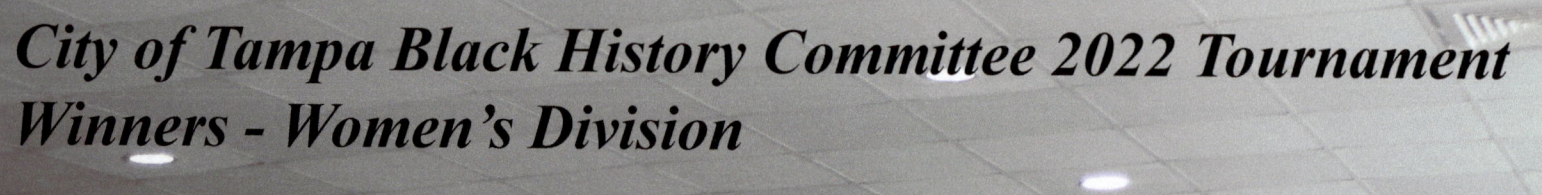

City of Tampa Black History Committee 2022 Tournament Winners - Women's Division

Lecretia Faulcon, Lavosha Jones, Jayla Williams, Geneala Broome

(Photos courtesy of Freddie Felder)

City of Tampa Black History Committee 2022 Tournament
Winners - Men's Division
Frank Woodard II, Lenzy Rhynes, Gary Green, Maurice House

(Photos courtesy of Freddie Felder)

(Photos courtesy of Freddie Felder)

(Photos courtesy of Freddie Felder)

The Food!

By Grace Griller

(Photos courtesy of Tony Caldwell)

Nilo Priede, Roger Priede, FA Priede, Angel Docubo, Founding group of the
Buster Agliano Tournament

Roger Priede, founder of the Buster
Tournament and major Rogers Park supporter.
Buster Tournament was the first major
fundraiser for First Tee

(Photos courtesy of Tony Caldwell)

Buster Agliano Tournament

George Shaw, Joe Robinson, Amos Hamilton, Bobbie Wilds

(Photos courtesy Tony Caldwell)

Joe Johnson, Jim Boynton, Sam Hunter annual supporters

Lavon Simmons (Photos courtesy Tony Caldwell)

Talladega College Golf Team
L to R: Herman Bryant, Travis Norman, Jim Dent, Jr., Wylie Tucker
(Athletic Directior), Alfred Baker (Golf Coach), V. Carnell McCray,
LeShea Owens
Members of the Talladega Golf Team that helped the school win the
1997 Minority Golf Championship in Clevenland Ohio.
All shown, except coaches, were part of Urban Jr. Golf Program at
Rogers Park Golf Course, a program ran by Mike Cooper for junior
golfers simular to the present-day First Tee program.

Class of 1964 Golf Team

Class of 2003 Golf Team

Calling All Golfers

(Field is limited to the first 100 Paid Players)

MIDDLETON SENIOR
HIGH SCHOOL ALUMNI
ASSOCIATION GOLF
SCHOLARSHIP FUNDRAISER

**October 22, 2022
Rogers Park Golf Course**
7910 N. 30th St., Tampa, Fl 33610

Shotgun Start 8:30am
son Scramble

For more i
Albert E. S
President
954-214

Middlet

Email
Webs
Address: Tile
Association, Inc.
P.O. Box 11463, Tampa, F

Almost fifty years of golf at Middleton and still counting

Annual Thanksgiving Dinner Giveaway for First Tee

This group help deliver up to 200 dinners for Thanksgiving.

Dinners were donated by a special friend and were distributed to needy families at Tampa Housing Authority and several local churches.

Shown L to R:
Rick Boniface
Tom Ellie
Melvin Blair
Lionel Ballard
India Banks
Steve Nesbitt
Ta'Shaney Barber
Dan Hughes
Robert Hyde
Joe Butler
Deina Nesbitt
Brad Janess

Hall of Famers

1986 - Harold Dunovant

1987 - Willie Black

1987 - Herman Dubois

1988 - Eldorado Long

1992 - Jim Dent

1995 - Rufus Lewis

1995 - Bobby Stroble

1998 - M.C. Wilder

1986 - Harold Dunovant

In 1986, Harold Dunovant, a black professional golfer, established the National Black Golf Hall of Fame "to recognize and honor the contributions of black golfers for their skills and to honor persons, regardless of race or ethnicity, who have done the most to promote golf in black communities." Mr. Dunovant was the first black person to graduate from the PGA's Business School and was finally elected to membership in the PGA of America in 1974. One of the 2008 Inductees was the Rogers Park Golf Course "for its historical role in providing a place where African-American golfers could enjoy the sport during the days of segregation."

1987 - Willie Black

Dedicated To
Pro Willie Black

(Courtesy of The Florida Sentinel News)

Willie Black was honored on July 3, 1994 by the Tampa Golf Club and Rogers Park Golf Course and unveiled by Manuel Wilder, Freddie Wilder, and Homer Hemingway.

The tribute proposed that: 1. The back 9 be named in his honor."The Willie Black Side." "The original 9 were carved out of the city dump into a beautiful course under Willie's direction. 2. A permanent statue/memorial be erected in the area of the #10 tee/clubhouse. 3. Renaming of 30th Street from Sligh north to the end of the street to Willie Black Drive

Items 2 and 3 were officially implemented. The back 9 is affectionately remembered as The Willie Black Side by those who remembers.

City Resolution No. 8580 was adopted by City Council and signed by Chairman, Joe Greco on April 14, 1994. City Councilman Perry C. Harvey, Jr. led the drive to get the street named in honor of Mr. Black. The Tampa Golf Club led the renaming effort and conducted the drive to erect the granite memorial.

Awards were also presented to "Pioneers of Golf" including Tampa's C. Blythe Andrews, Jr., Clarence Green, and Raymond Dix.[16]

The inscription reads: Willie Black Side
Honoring the late Willie Black, Sr. for his dedication and contributions to golf and development of Rogers Park Golf Course. 1994

1992 - Jim Dent

James Lacey Dent was born in the golf mecca of Augusta, Georgia, home of the Masters Tournament, though as an African American he wouldn't have been allowed onto the Augusta National course at the time, except as a caddie. He caddied both at Augusta National and at Augusta Country Club as a youth. Dent attended Augusta's historically black Paine College.

Dent turned pro in 1966. During his regular (under 50) career he was Florida PGA Champion three times. However he is mainly notable for his success on the Senior PGA Tour (now Champions Tour), where he won 12 tournaments between 1989 and 1998. Known for his driving ability, Dent was in 1974 the inaugural winner of the World Long Drive Championship and would go on to retain the title in 1975.

Developing Future Legends

**YMCA Urban Junior Golf
The First Tee of Tampa Bay**

The First Tee of Tampa Bay is an extension of YMCA Urban Junior Golf, a program of the Tampa Metropolitan Area YMCA. The origin of the program dates back to 1991, when it began as Urban Junior Golf. The original organization was founded by local golf professional Mike Cooper. Mike was a product of a junior golf program in Chicago, IL, and wanted to bring a similar concept to the Tampa Bay community. This concept was to offer affordable and accessible golf opportunities to children from moderate socio-economic backgrounds, and to use the inherent social and recreational values associated with the game to shape the lives of each participant.

Urban Junior Golf first used Persimmon Hills Golf Course for its home. The site was a nine-hole executive golf course and driving range located on 56th street, just south of Hillsborough. No longer in operation, the original site served as the headquarters until 1993 when (then) County Commissioner Sylvia Kimball spoke to the Tampa Sports Authority (TSA) on behalf of the organization. She expressed the needs and good deeds of the program, and convinced the TSA to allow Rogers Park Golf Course to serve as the new site. All believed that the Rogers Park community perfectly fit the desired model. The staff at Rogers Park GC was already providing considerable expertise by-way of golf lessons, time, and limited access. The entire community would now begin to regard Rogers as the center of youth golf activities, and the reputation spread rapidly. As enrollment increased, so did the operational demands. The organization began to grow and a Board of Directors was created. Corporate and individual donations slowly matriculated, and the United States Golf Association (USGA) became a regular grantor. One of the first USGA grants was to initiate and implement a Caddie Club, which provided training and temporary jobs to teenaged members. The Caddie Club was launched at Rogers Park in 1993, but grew more once it shifted to Palma Ceia Country Club in 1994-95. The initiative became cumbersome to continue, however, due to lack of staffing and adequate training systems. It ceased all-together when the private club closed for renovation, yet the relationships and visibility gained helped catapult the program in terms of purpose,

Michael Cooper and Cole (Photo Courtesy of Michael Cooper)

worthiness, and recognition. This reputation was also greatly enhanced by the on-going lesson programs, tournament schedule, scholarship assistance, and community partnerships.

Urban Junior Golf became an official program of the Tampa Metropolitan Area YMCA in January 1998. This provided much needed administrative support and marketability. The First Tee was announced at approximately the same time, and immediate efforts were made to become an official Chapter. The mindset (then) was that the once small Urban Junior Golf programs would now be aligned with the largest and (perhaps) most influential community based youth organization in Tampa Bay (Tampa YMCA), as well as a national organization created by the five leaders within the golf industry. The First Tee would soon become the most recognized youth golf organization on a global basis. The sudden popularity seemed to be reaching a crescendo, and it appeared as if the Tampa YMCA might even gain full operational reins of Rogers Park GC in 1999.

The possibility of operating Rogers Park GC was actually proposed by the TSA. Their belief, at the time, was that Rogers Park was deteriorating in playing conditions and in need of major renovation. They also believed that sufficient capital dollars were unavailable for the project, and that shifting managerial controls to a not-for-profit youth agency might be the answer. The idea of the managerial shift found opposition before the concept could be fully explored, however. Renovation dollars for Rogers Park were eventually provided by the City of Tampa, and YMCA Urban Junior Golf moved its headquarters to Terrace Hill Golf Club during the renovation period.

The Rogers Park renovation stirred quite a debate throughout the entire Tampa Bay community. One of the outcomes for the youth golf program was a heightened awareness. Soon, community partnerships included the Parks & Recreation Department for Tampa and Hillsborough County, the Boys & Girls Club, and the Tampa Housing Authority. Financial support was provided by several other local civic organizations, including the Northwest Optimist Club, the Tampa Sports Club, the Gary Koch Foundation, and PGA Tour events. Enrollment sky-rocketed to over 1000 participants each year, and national support continued from the USGA, PGA, and The First Tee. The decision was made to maintain headquarters at Terrace Hill GC and a Learning Center and short-game area was created specifically for participants. Programs and enrollment has remained consistent through recent years, and the community has come to expect and support summer camps at up to six Tampa Bay golf locations, and on-going year round activities at Terrace Hill.

Recently, the group has been presented with an opportunity to add Rogers Park Golf Course as an additional dedicated site. Rogers Park is located within the Tampa Enterprise Zone, in zip code area 33610. This community is identified as having the highest percentage of minority residents in Hillsborough County. Moreover, structured youth development and/or after-school programs are scarce. By making Rogers Park a second site, The First Tee of Tampa Bay will enhance its tradition of providing a place to grow for children and creating opportunities through the game of golf. These opportunities not only include the chance to learn the game that lasts a lifetime; but to participate in a proven youth development program featuring life skills and positive development. These opportunities come from trained coaches and a structured certification process. Participants also have a chance to participate in The First Tee National Academy at Kansas State University and earn college scholarships; both life-enhancing benefits of The First Tee. To-date, The First Tee of Tampa Bay has sent approximately two-dozen teenagers to the National Academy, and had four members earn The First Tee Scholars awards.

First Tee, as an international youth development organization, introduces the game of golf and it's inherent values to young people. Through after school and in school programs, they help shape the lives of young people from all walks of life by reinforcing values like integrity, respect, and perseverance through the game of golf. First Tee - Tampa Bay is the leading organization for youth for Junior Golf in Tampa.

First Tee provides golf and life skill programs, such as Group Lessons, LPGA Girls Golf, Summer camps, Team, Players' Club and a Tournament Series. These programs are held at many supporting locations that support Junior Golf in Tampa.

Their Group Lesson program, their core program, provides golf instruction and life skills to juniors ages 5 to 18. Their Players' Club is a program specific specifically designed for high school players that are active in Tampa Junior Golf, either through their high school team or local golf team.

Their LPGA Girls golf program delivers life skills and many other values that are built through camaraderie among the girls via focused activities.

The Summer Camps are open to any player aged 5 to 18 and is available to beginners and advanced players who would like to be involved with Junior Golf in Tampa. These week-long camps cover all aspects of the game, with instruction given by golf professionals and certified first team staff.

In October 2013, Norman Black, a then junior at Chamberlain High School and a First Tee student, made history as the first African American to ever win the coveted District Golf Championship title. It was not his first tournament, however, according to his mother, Carla Levy, by then Norman had won three major tournaments.

Mackenzie Mack is a competitor, a teacher and student when it comes to the game of golf. As a competitor, Mackenzie has played at the most elite levels of the game against some of the best in the world. As a junior golfer Mackenzie played for and was a member of the following tours: the American Junior Golf Association (AJGA), the International Junior Golf Tour (IJGT), Teens on the Green and Western States Golf Association (WSGA). Mackenzie also enjoyed the honor of competing for: the Tiger Woods Junior Golf Team for 3 years, the Girls America Cup team for Southern Nevada for four years and the First Tee of Southern Nevada in the First Tee Open at Pebble Beach two years in a row. Also during her junior career, Mackenzie was recognized as one of GolfWeek's top 100 junior golfers in the country.

After achieving a stellar junior golf career, Mackenzie was awarded a full golf scholarship to Indiana State University (ISU) where Mackenzie was the first black woman to compete as a member of the Women's Golf Team. Mackenzie graduated from ISU in 2010 with a major in Marketing and minors in Finance and Spanish and achieved magna cum laude honors. Mackenzie also received a Master's in Business Administration (MBA) from the ISU Scott College of Business in 2011. During her time at Indiana State, Mackenzie spent one season as the ISU Women's Golf Team Assistant Coach and co-founded a non-profit organization called Tee it Up, Inc. Tee it Up was a means of growing the game of golf and sharing her passion with underserved communities. In 2011, Tee it Up was awarded a grant that allowed Mackenzie and her team to teach golf to kids in Bitburg, Germany.

As a student of the game, Mackenzie has perfected her craft by becoming a teaching professional member of the LPGA Professionals and PGA of America. Mackenzie is TPI Certified, US Kids Certified, First Tee Certified, and PGA Hope Certified. Mackenzie has also held status on both the Suncoast Ladies and LPGA Symetra Tours.

As a teacher, Mackenzie was the Senior Program Director for the First Tee of Tampa Bay that reached over 70,000 students each year, Associate Executive Director of The First Tee of Tennessee in Memphis that generated over 1600 junior golf rounds played in 2020, and was the US Kids Local Tournament Director that had over 900 registrations and had 13 students

Mackenzie Mack Professional Golfer

qualify and participate in US Kids Worlds and Teen Worlds in 2020.

Mackenzie was recently the FIRST selected to Callaway Golf Company's Leadership Rotational Program at their worldwide headquarters in Carlsbad, California. The program is designed to provide exceptional industry leaders with hands-on manufacturing/ retail experience across various Callaway business units as well as one-on-one coaching/mentorship with the goal of cultivating the next generation of leadership at Callaway Golf Company.

Dr. Mike Cooper, Executive
Director First Tee

Rev. Thomas Scott,
City Councilman

Gary Kock PGA Golfer/ NBC Golf Channel Announcer, Lisa Crow The First
Tee of Tampa Bay Board Member, Ian Baxter The First Tee of Tampa Bay
Executive Director

Jeff Leonard, Program/Executive Director First Tee Tampa
Bay

April 2009 - First Tee opening Day

Joe Barrow President/CEO of
First Tee   Son of Joe Louis

Tom Looby, CEO
of Tampa YMCA

Raheem Morris Tampa Bay Buccaneers
head coach from 2009 to 2011

Mentor Group 2011 Mentees: Edward Bright, Cortine Culpepper, Ciera Culpepper, James Mayhue, Jaiden Champman, Ibree Fleming, Aniya Fleming, Martell Flemng. Marqiose Fleming

Mentoring Program

Mentoring Group was formed by a group of friends. By using The First Tee 9 core values: Respect, courtesy, Responsibility, Honesty, Sportmanship, Confidence, Judgement, Perserverance, Integrity. They meet two times a month and cover topics such as time management, career opportunities, financal planning, health care, nutrition, and mental health. They provide knowledge and personal life experience, to help these young kids grow and develop into productive citizens.

Lionel and Guest Speaker at Fundraiser dinner - Jack Nicklaus

Mentor Group 2011 Mentors: Larry Hodge, Kat Lewis, Dr. Pat Dupar, Chaunicia Willis, Cheryl Johnson, Jennifer Seay, Lionel Ballard, Renita Crosby, Leon williams, Nicole Newcomb, Joe Butler. Not shown: Ted Sparks

The Legends

L-R James Black, Charlie Owens, Calvin Peete, Jim Dent

The Four Legends Clinic
4/28/13

Standing: Charlie Owens, Kennie Sims, Jerry Bruner, Jeffery Donovant, Jim Dent
Sitting: James Black

April 28, 2013

Non Golf Pro Legends Who Played at Rogers

*They golfed for inspiration and are movers and shakers
in their chosen professions*

Perry A. Little, On September 21st, 1977, Perry Little was appointed to the County Court for the 13th Judicial Circuit by Governor Ruben Askew. Judge Little is one of only two African Americans to be appointed a judge in Hillsborough County, Florida. Judge Little presided as a traffic court judge and county court judge for more than twelve years. Then on December 6, 1993, Judge Little was appointed to the Circuit Court by Governor Lawton Chiles. There, Judge Little served in the Juvenile and Circuit Civil divisions. [17]

John Burke Jr. "Sarge" logged 22.5 Years of service. He served as a part of the 82nd Airborne with the following medals: CMAT Badge; silver Star; 2 Bronze Star (WV); Air Metal; 6 Army Commendation; 2 Vador; 4 Purple Heart; 3 Tours in Vietnam (in combat)

Dr. Leonard Campbell
Educator

Carl Edward Everett III is a former Major League Baseball outfielder. He played for eight teams over the course of a 14-year career. He was a member of the Chicago White Sox when they won the 2005 World Series. He threw right-handed and played all outfield positions, and occasionally designated hitter. Everett attended Hillsborough High School in Tampa, Florida and was a letterman in football, baseball, and track.

Jay McNair receiving winner's honors from Doug Williams at the Doug Williams Tournament

Douglas Williams, football executive, former quarterback, and coach. During Super Bowl XXII Washington Redskins against the Denver Broncos, he was named Super Bowl MVP after passing for 340 yards and four touchdowns, a single-quarter Super Bowl record which he set in the second quarter, making him the first black quarterback to both start and win a Super Bowl.

Former quarterback and team executive for the Tampa Bay Buccaneers

James Boynton Jr.
Former Assistant Attorney General State of Florida

Rev. John Milton Rutledge was a resident in Tampa for over 30 years. He served in the Army Air Corp during WWII. He received the call to ministry in 1961, and following in his father's footsteps, connected with the African Methodist Episcopal Church becoming an ordained elder. "Rev.," as he was affectionately known, pastored AME churches in Florida which included Apalachicola, Milton, Lynn Haven, Port St. Joe and churches in Green Cove Springs and Ormond Beach before being assigned to Mt. Olive AME Tampa. His tenure in Tampa lasted 21 years he retired in 2002.

Marvin Knight, owner of the Oriental Fish Market and TECO retiree. He has a degree in electronic technology and computer electronics. Mr. Knight is very active in the community and is a member of the West Tampa CRA, HART Board member, and Freddie Solomon Boys and Girls Club.

NFL Hall Of Famer **Derrick Brooks** football linebacker who played in the National Football League (NFL) for 14 seasons with the Tampa Bay Buccaneers. Brooks played college football at Florida State, where he twice received consensus All-American honors, and was selected by the Buccaneers in the first round of the 1995 NFL Draft. An 11-time Pro Bowl selection and five-time first-team All-Pro, Brooks was the NFL Defensive Player of the Year in 2002 en route to winning the franchise's first Super Bowl title in Super Bowl XXXVII.

Brian Garman - University of Tampa Professor

NFL Hall of Famer *Ricky Jackson* played in the National Football League (NFL) for the New Orleans Saints (1981–1993) and the San Francisco 49ers (1994–1995). With the Saints, he led the team's Dome Patrol linebacker corps. In 1997, Jackson was inducted into the New Orleans Saints Hall of Fame. He won a Super Bowl ring with the 49ers in Super Bowl XXIX one year before retiring.

This is the look of joy after former **Mayor Pam Iorio** made her first birdie. She now loves golf and here's what she said about Rogers Park: "There's no golf course I enjoy more than Roger's Park. Maybe it's the camaraderie or the sense of history. It is where I can relax and know I am amongst friends. The course itself is beautiful, but the people make it unforgettable."

In 1985, at age 26, Pam Iorio became the youngest person ever elected to the Hillsborough County Commission. She served as Supervisor of Elections for Hillsborough County for ten years. During the 2000 presidential election recount, she was the president of the State Association of County Elections Supervisors propelling her into the role of spokesperson. On April 1, 2003, she was sworn in as Mayor of Tampa, becoming the second woman to hold the office.

Gary Sheffield, former professional baseball outfielder who played in Major League Baseball for eight teams from 1988 to 2009. He is a sports agent.
For most of his career, Sheffield played right field, though he has also played left field, third base, shortstop, and a handful of games at first base. He played for the Milwaukee Brewers, San Diego Padres, Florida Marlins, Los Angeles Dodgers, Atlanta Braves, New York Yankees, Detroit Tigers, and the New York Mets. Sheffield was a first-round pick of the Brewers, who selected him sixth overall in the 1986 amateur draft after a standout prep career at Hillsborough High School in Tampa, Florida. As a Florida Marlin, he received a World Series Ring in 1997.

Associated Organizations

The Smith Family
The Hamilton Family
The Tampa Golf Club 1980
Women of Color Golf
Black Jewels
Par & Bogey Club
Roger's Park Men's Association
Saturday's Men Group
Tuesday & Thursday Men's Group

The Smith Family

Smith Brothers and Lionel Ballard From left: Albert Smith, Lionel Ballard, Herbert Smith, Eddie Smith, Sammie Smith, Aaron Smith, and Stanley Smith (Inlay: David Smith). The Smith brothers & Middleton High school graduates represented their family and school well.

The Hamilton Family

Hamilton Brothers From left: Charles, Kenneth, Amos, Willie, and Ralph

The Hamilton Family

Charlie Hamilton, known around the golf course as "Sneaky Pro", was the patriarch of the Hamilton Family Golfers. A father and his sons.

Charlie Hamilton, Charles Hamilton

Amos Hamilton

Charles, Kenneth, & Amos Hamilton

Charles Hamilton

Charles, Willie, & Amos Hamilton

The Tampa Golf Club 1980

Front row: Marvin Bradford, D.S. Gilly, Archie Mond, Willie McCrimmon
Back row: Harold Lee, Robert Sutton, Rufus Lewis, Frank Branga, Kinsey, Arthur Smith (Courtesy Rufus Lewis)

In 1975, Francis Davis had a vision. He saw a golf organization in Tampa. Florida, that would promote the positive aspects of golf and help youngsters by providing leadership and financial assistance for college. That organization would also sponsor tournaments, which would serve to fund the youth programs.

Davis was interested in forming a golf organization, but did not know how to put it together. He believed he was led by God to do this. God showed him. To look among the players for leaders. He picked the officers from among them, and the organization exploded.

In 1975, Tampa International Golf League was organized, and later that year it was. It blossomed into the Tampa Golf Club Two, and incorporated, nonprofit organization. Also in 1975, but TGC organized a 4th of July golf tournament, called the Bicentennial Golf Classic. The classic kept the name until 1977, when it was renamed the All-American Amateur Golf Classic, which is held annually at Rogers Park Golf Course.

The charter members of the club at that time were: Frances Davis, Marvin Bradford, D. S. Gilley, Randolph Kinsey, Harold Lee, Willie McCrimmon, Billy Mitchell and Howard Pierce.

These members started out meeting at each other's homes until the membership grew to about 25 members. The new members were Louis H Carter, Archie Mond., Richard. London, Arthur Smith, Gainous. Byron, Bob Moore, John Kinsey, Freddie Sterling, Herbert Fisher, Equilla Davis, Wayne Brookins, Charlie White, Rufus Lewis, Robert Sutton., James Young, Randolph Smith, Charlie Tolliver, Benny Milford, Leonard Campbell Collins, Ted Brown, Willie Black and Arlanders Alford. The membership is made up of large number of active golfers and is a part of the statewide organization, the Sunshine State Amateur Golfers Association.

The Black Jewels Ladies Golf Association of Florida

Nikki Gaskin-Capehart
Area President 2009-2011

*T*he Black Jewels Ladies Golf Association of Florida (BJLGA) was established in 2008 by Rasheena Wilson, founding association president, naming Lorain Williams as the founding president of the local chapter. BJLGA of Florida covers the entire state of Florida. The BJLGA chapter to cover an entire state.

BJLGA of Florida is a 501 (c) 3 organization whose mission focuses on encouraging women of color and young girls to (1) enjoy helathy personal development and relationships through golf programs; (2) participate in the game of golf by providing golf clinics, golf skill and instructions, and opportunities of athletic development and competition; and (3) enjoy mentoring opportunties provided through BJLGA of Florida's mentoring program.

Black Jewels Ladies'Golf Association of Florida Officers:
Nikki Gaskin-Capehart
Renita D. Crosby
Louise Gaskin
Lynette Darrell
Tommye Brown
Jennifer Seay
Loretta F. Murray

Members:
Gina Booker
April Harley
Cheryl Johnson
D. Shenell Reed
Daina Troupe
Chauncia Willis

D. Shenell Reed, Cheryl Johnson, Lynette Darrell,
Jennifer Seay, Renita D. Crosby, Chauncia Willis

Women of Color Golf

Clemmie Perry, Founder and Executive Director of Women of Color Golf (WOCG) & Girls On the Green Tee (GOTGT) programs

Women of Color Golf (WOCG) members: Vasti Amaroa, Kenneshia Martin, Monica Solomon, Robyn Thompson, Lynne Morgana

Clemmie Perry is the Founder and Executive Director of Women of Color Golf (WOCG) & Girls On the Green Tee (GOTGT) programs. The mission of Women of Color Golf is to promote and facilitate the inclusion of minority women, girls and communities of color into game of golf. This inspiration is then turned into action with organized golf clinics, recreational golf events, business networking & mentoring opportunities. WOCG is not-for-profit organization that started in 2014, and has introduced more than 800 minority women & girls in the basic fundamentals of golf in Tampa Bay, St. Petersburg, and Washington, D.C.

The Women of Color Golf (WOCG) and Girls on the Green Tee (GOTGT) initiatives have grown into a nationally recognized community program with recognition by former President Barack Obama, as a United States White House as Champions of Change for After School Programs for Marginalized Girls. WOCG has partnered with Rogers Park Golf Course for several social and networking events, to expose the community to the rich history of the golf course and its many legends.

WOCG has been featured on The Golf Channel, CNN International, Forbes, Ebony, Black Enterprise, Onyx Magazine, Golf for Her, Professional Golf Association (PGA) magazine, the African American Golfer's Digest and several local media broadcasts.[18]

Benita Maynor
Professional Golfer

Benita Maynor

Benita Maynor was born and raised in Tampa Florida and although her travels has taken her many places, her roots has always been in Tampa, Florida. Benita has had a full career though out her life, holding many positions where the majority of her professional career was spent working at GTE Communications and GTE Data Services serving he Black Jewels Ladies Golf Association of Florida was established in 2008 by Rasheena Wilson, Founding President of Black Jewels Ladies Golf Association - naming Lorain Willaims as the Founding President of the local chapter. BJLGA of Florida covers the entire state of Florida. The only one to cover the entire state at that time. in managerial and leadership positions.

Benita was introduced to the game of golf by her father later in life, she fell in love with the game and started playing competitively with the Sunshine State Amateur Golfers Association where she traveled throughout the state of Florida competing and taking many first place wins and close seconds.

In the year 2000, she decided to challenge herself even more and applied to play in the SBC Professional Qualifying Golf Tournament as an amateur and made the cut. She gained conditional status on that tour. The SBC Futures Tour is the Ladies Professional Golf Association (LPGA) Developmental tour.

Since that decision, she has had many wonderful opportunities to work in the golf industry. She worked in the Pro shop at Rogers Park Golf Course and coordinated outside clubhouse events for the establishment, she served as Executive Assistant under Michael Cooper, then the Director of First Tee Southeast Region, served as assistant to the VP of Golf Operations, Kennie Sims with the Tampa Sports Authority.

Still while performing those duties, she managed to qualify for the WSGT tour (Women's Senior Professional Golf Tour) where she competed. [19]

Benita Maynor and Calvin Pete

Darlene Hale
Professional Golfer

Darlene Hale was born and raised in Tampa, Florida where she enjoyed playing many sports. In fact, she was All County in basketball and track and field for three consecutive years at Jefferson High School and earned a full four-year basketball scholarship to Texas Southern University located in Houston, Texas. While attending T.S.U. Darlene earned the honor and an N.A.I.A. Basketball - All American. She graduated with a BA degree in Accounting. However the athlete didn't start playing golf until she was 30 years old, this happened after seeing NBA great Michael Jordan play golf. Darlene received her first pair of golf shoes and an 8 iron from her sister Joy, for her 30th birthday.

She turned pro in 1999. She competed as often as her busy schedule allowed. She played on several mini-tours (futures tour a/k/a DURAMED Tour, The Next Generation Tour and The Suncoast Tour). She didn't stop there, she also competed in several state opens from 2011 to 2021.

* Georgia Women's Open - Place 1st twice & 2nd once
* Tennessee Women's Open - Placed 2nd
* Ohio Women's Open - Place 3rd
* Florida Women's Open - Placed 6th in 2019
* 2021 Senior Pro Division - Placed first

The tournament was contested at Riomar County Club, Vero Beach, Florida, August 6 - 8, 2021. Darlene is very thankful for the support from her sponsor "Titleist", she has believed in her for over two decades. She would also like to thank those who have spent countless number of hours with sharpening her skills (Jim Dent, Sr., P.G.A. Tour player, Keven Blair, USGA Teacher, and Julius Richardson (deceased) USGA teacher).

Taking risk in life always comes with wondering what happens if you fail. But without taking a risk, one will never know. For Darlene Hale, she sought out her dreams in golf and never looked back.

Today, Darlene Hale serves as a prime role model and is leading the way in showing everyone that obtaining success as a black person in predominately "white man's game" is possible. Hale particularly seeks to encourage youth of all persuasions on the opportunities and benefits of playing golf.

Darlene, along with being a golf professional, is and astute business woman who owns and operates the Rainbow of Kids Academy - "Caring for Our Future", SDA Enterprises, LLC - a Real Estate Investment Company and her 501 (3)(c) Non Profit business Birdie Babe, Inc., established "To Empower Families through Our Youth". As you can see, Darlene is a pillar in her community, educating lives, providing homes and strengthening families.

Busy and productive, Darlene's favorite quote is: "I Can Do All Things Through Christ Who Strengthens Me." (Philippians 4:13). [20]

Charles L. Hamilton Professional Golfer

Charles L. Hamilton was born and raised in Walterboro, SC. He later moved to Tampa, FL in 1965. He is the son of Charlie Hamilton AKA "Sneaky Pro" and (late)Thelma Hamilton (Stephens). Charles learned to play golf he was 11 years old, his father Charlie taught him everything about the game of golf.

He attended Blake High School were he won his first golf tournament in 1967. This was the first championship Blake ever won for the game of golf. This was proud moment for the school and most Africans Americans because golf wasn't a recognized sport for African Americans. By winning the first ever championship for Blake this brought much attention to Charles and the school.

The late Willie Black (Head Pro at Rogers Park) gifted Charles with a nice set of golf clubs as token of him being proud of him. In 1970, Charles won the Mid-Winter Pro/Amateur Tournament. Dr. Andrews hosted golf tournaments from 1979-1980, in hopes of getting African American golfers together to play golf and bond with one another. Charles was able to win 4 out 10 tournaments held by Dr. Andrews making it a notable mention amongst the African American Community.

In 1981, former Pittsburgh Steelers Glen Edwards hosted his own tournament resulting in Charles being the winner of the tournament. He worked for Palma Ceia Golf and Country Club for over 40 years, where he won golf tournaments in 2003, 2004 and 2006. He was well known around the golf course for being one of the best players who ever played the game of golf. He was often sought out for his advice and private golf lessons.

Charles retired from Palma Ceia in 2016. He is married to Bonnie Hamilton for 49 years. He has three children and six grandchildren. He takes proud in caring for his 91 year old father. He continues to play the game of golf every opportunity he gets and spends quality time enjoying his family and friends.

21

The Tuesday & Thursday Men's Group

These golfers have routinely competed every Tuesday and Thursday over the last 25 years at Rogers Park Course.

Left to Right as shown:
Earnest Chester
Thomas Gillard Jr.
Tony Marion
Michael Watson
Joseph Bell I
Sherman Charter I
Cedric Robinson Jr.

Not Shown:
Jasper Jolly
Luther Rogers
Luterric Colbert
Nat James
Starlin Martin
Harold Watson
Rozier Pearson
Arlander Alford
Curtis Green

Par and Bogie Golf Club

At any given time, as a club, Par and Bogie Golf Club had other golfers playing with us. We played all over the seven counties, some before they had a club house.

Founded in 1988, the club had golfers from Cuba, Haiti, Jamaica, Canada, New York, Ohio, Michigan, Hawaii, New Orleans and of course, Florida. Par & Bogie received the Outstanding Leaders in Golf from the African American Culture Digest in 2011

They made history in 1991 when Par & Bogie Golf Club became the first club to have men and women as members of the same club.

Ruth Ouderkirk, Coretta Johnson, Dorthy McHenry, Novella Campbell
Back row" Williams Saunders, John Byrd

Founding Board:
Ruth Ouderkirk
Coretta Johnson
Dorthy McHenry
Novella Campbell

First President: William Saunders
Brenda Stillings
John Byrd
Ian Leotard
Duport Fennell
Madelyn McClendon

Rupert Fennell, Brenda Stillings, Julius Hanns, Victor Fegurson, Lennard Campbell

John Byrd and founding president William Saunders

Golfers beware! If you approach the rock the wrong way, you may just run up on an alliagator coming up for a mid-day snack. This collection of rocks reminds golfers of an emerging alliagator.

Courtesy of the Florida Sentinel

Sentinel Bulletin

FRIDAY, NOVEMBER 1, 1991   **48 PAGES**   **PRICE 47¢ +**

▼▼▼▼▼▼▼▼▼▼

Par And Bogie Club Is First Of Its Kind

(SEE STORY ON PAGE 11-A)

Par & Bogie Golf Club— First Of Its Kind

BY LEON CREWS
Sentinel Staff Writer

New to the area, the Par and Bogie Golf Club is the first club to have men and women as members of the same club.

Cretta Johnson, president of the club, says, "We have golfers representing all levels of play, from beginners to A players."

Johnson, who is also the Director of Equal Opportunity and Human Relations for Hillsborough County, helped organize the club three years ago. "Myself, along with John Byrd, who was the club's first president, William Saunders, Madelyn McClendon and Dorothy McHenry put the club together in 1988. Since

CRETTA JOHNSON

then, membership has grown to 20, with the recent addition of two new members.

"To become a member of the club," says Johnson, "approach a member for spon-

sorship, a recommendation is made that you be accepted for membership and the club votes on it. We are looking for people who enjoy the game but don't take it so seriously."

With Johnson's responsibilities as EEOC Director, it's tough to devote as much time to the club as she would like. "Many of our members are retired and have time to devote to activities planned by the club."

According to Johnson, the ratio of men to women is basically even. "That's what makes this club so unique. Most of the members belong to Rogers Park so that would be considered our home course."

Some of the other officers of the club are Ruth Ouderkirk, Vice President; John Byrd,

Secretary and Charles Thomas, Treasurer. "Most of the members are a group of people that met on the golf course," says Johnson. "We are all basically new to Florida as we have only been here for a little more than 5 years."

The club has Kenneth Syms, Rogers Park Pro, working with some of the members and participates in their youth clinics. "We sponsor minority youth who are unable to pay their clinic donations," quips Johnson. "We try to provide as much encouragement to minority youth as we can to get them involved in the game of golf."

Johnson proudly proclaims that she has been playing golf for 22 years now. "My brothers used to caddy in Leesville, Louisiana and they used to bring discarded clubs from the country club because blacks couldn't play there. We would convert the school yard into a golf course and get at it. I have three brothers who are great golfers."

Johnson feels that the expense of becoming a golfer can be dealt with. "Through programs sponsored by Mike Cooper and other black professionals, kids can still experience the joys of the game without incurring the expense."

"Black people need to know this is a sport they can participate in. The more blacks become involved in the sport, the more we will see on a professional tour and on television."

Roger's Park Men's Group

The men's group was started primarily by two men. Burl Bolesta and Bobby Dunn.

They originally played at Rocky Point for several years in the late 70s. When Rocky Point was being renovated, they started playing at Rogers Park and liked the course in the early 80s.

The group consisted of men from all walks of life ranging from age 30-70. They played every Saturday and Sunday mornings. Saturday was individual play including a skins game and more. On Sunday they played a scramble having the captains (A players) pick their team in front of the clubhouse.

Acy Jeffcoat and Sam Dillon - both of whom still play on Sunday, were in charge of scoring and maintaining player handicaps. Sam was even taught the game of golf by Bobby Dunn.

The Men's Group was comprised of about 40 players on the weekends. They all came out for the love of golf and the competition it provided. There were several single digit handicappers in the group which made the game quite competitive. Many times 18 holes was not enough golf for some of the guys and 9 or 18 more holes would occur on may weekends. They would re-choose teams and play until dark.

The group has dwindled over the years - due to players passing away, health issues, moving out of the area, etc.

There are only a few players left that still play on Sunday.

Acy Jeffcoat, Sam Dillon, Emerson Decker and Becky Miles (who they allowed to play back in the early 80s because her husband Robbie played with the Men's group. She had to play from the Men's tee back then. Now all of the remaining players play the senior tees and women's tee.

Golf was the game that brought all these men together and forged life-long friendships. They played for the love of the game.[22]

Front row L-R Mike Smith, unkn, Andy Fotopolous, Jay Murpay, Tom Mansavage, unkn
Back row: Unkn, Paul Fowler, ukn, Jim Murphy, Mario Agoila, Acy Seffcoat, Jim Tapp, Robert Tapp, Chuck Davis, Carl Ackerman, Teddy Fotopolous
Players not shown in photo:
Burl Bolesta, Bobby Dunn, Les Decker, Vern Smith, Ed Bradburn, John Bradburn, Jerry Langston, Sam Slaughter, Carl Ackerman, John Ackerman, Jimmy Fotopolous, Teddy Fotopolous, Jack Holt, Max Castro, Dr. Fred Peterson, Dr. Chuck Kiss, Steve Allinder, Ed Reynolds, Earl Turner, Norwood Britt, Al Lucus, Robbie Miles, Emerson Decker

The Saturday Men's Group

Since 1987, historic Roger's Park Golf Course has been the mecca for a group of distinguished men that challenge the course and each other. What's remarkable about this group is they have never miss a Saturday morning tee time.

Ray Peters, Lou Colbert, Joe Sykes, and two high school principals were the founding fathers of the golf network.

Over the years, Peters has continued this golf network legacy, friendships, competitive golf and laughs. The core group has expanded with the addition of Clyde Bunch, Ray Campbell and Freddy Felder. Special thanks to Clyde and Ray who ensures the group's Saturday morning tee times.

The group welcomes all players, regardless of their handicaps. Players come and go, but on a normal Saturday, twelve players show up to play. Some players are from the Bay Area and other players are new to Tampa Bay looking for a game.

23

Brandon (First Timer) Freddy Varner, Lanny Sumpter, Ray Peters, Freddie Felder, Clyde Bunch, Larry Shipp, J.B. Brown
Not shown: Don Southall, Ray Campbell, Michael Reeves, Dr. Donald Phillips

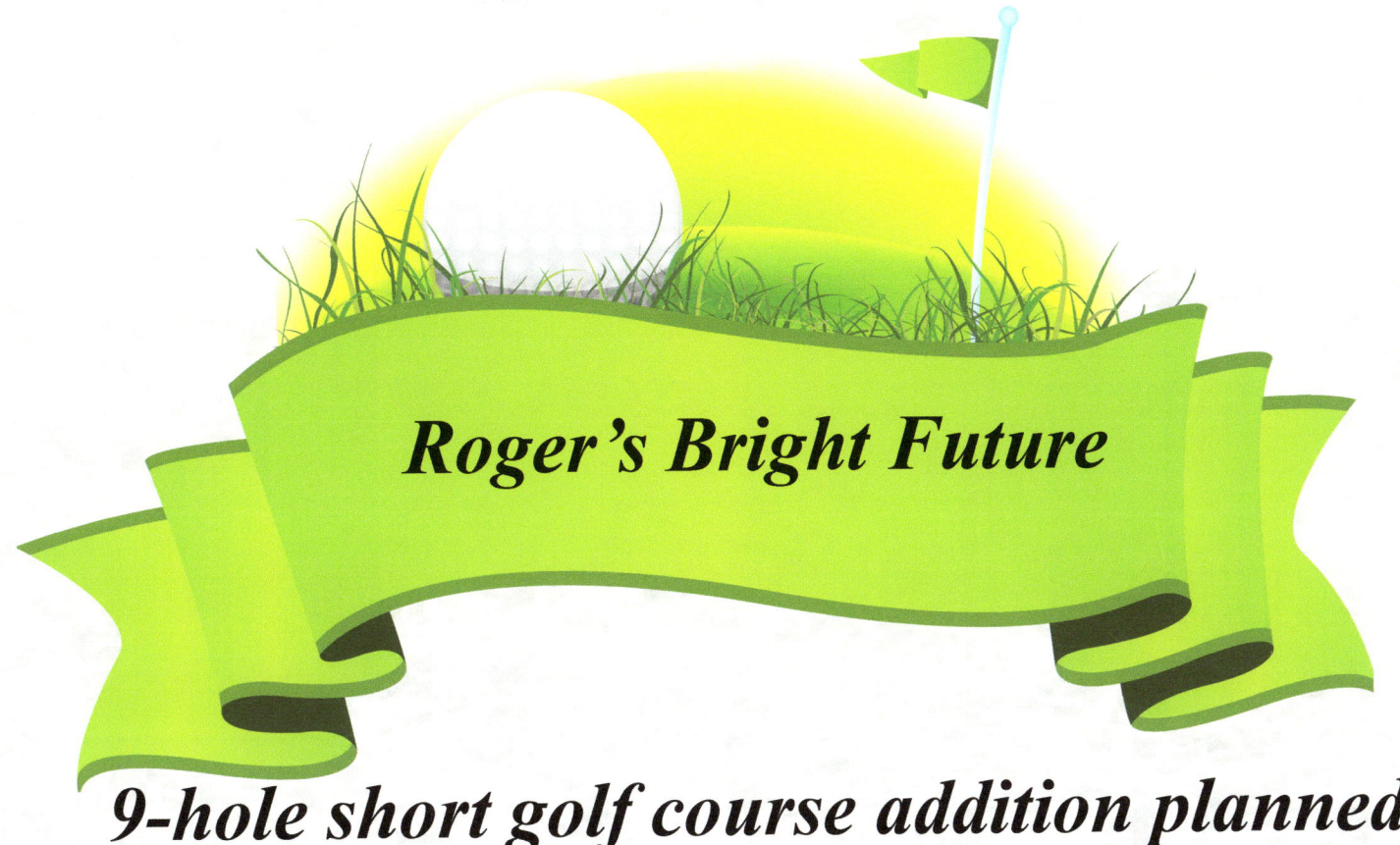

Roger's Bright Future

9-hole short golf course addition planned

In 2022, the First Tee – Tampa Bay is partnering with the Tampa Sports Authority to design and build a 9-hole short golf course at Rogers Park Golf Course. The short course would consist of holes ranging from approximately 60 to 120 yards in length, utilizing the land that sits between the 12th, 13th, 16th and 17th holes of the current Rogers Park 18-hole course. The short course at Rogers Park has been designed by renowned golf course architect Steve Smyers and will be built by ABM construction during the summer and fall of 2022. The short course will have natural fairways and greens, and artificial tee boxes to help reduce the wear and tear that comes with course play. When complete, the short course will be open to the public for a nominal fee when not being used for First Tee – Tampa Bay youth programming.

First Tee-
Tampa Bay
Rogers Park
Short Course

Tampa, Florida

LEGEND:

Green
Fairway
Tees
Bunkers
Slopes & Mounds
Areas of Earthwork

SCALE: 1" = 50'

MARCH 17, 2022

1 - Construction Plans

Based on preliminary community briefings at time of print, this is the designated area for the expansion

Appendix

Endnote information and photos submitted with permission to print by:

1   (James Ransom, grandson of the G.D. Rogers, Sr. on behalf of the Rogers Family)
2   James Ransom
3   Submitted for inclusion with promission to print by
4   Albert Smith
5   Mary E James
6   Bettye Davis
7   Florida Sentinel Bulletin, 2/6/2009 First Woman Golfer At Rogers Park Played With 2 Clubs
8   Kaye Andrews
9   Kennie Sims
10   Larry Brunner
11   Bill Gainer
12   Vince Reid
13   T.J. Heidel
14   Herbert Smith
15   Florida Sentinel Bulletin
16   Florida Sentinel Bulletin 1994 "Legendary Golfer Honored With Street In His Name
17   Perry Little
18   Clemmie Perry
19   Benita Manor
20   Darlene Hale
21   Charles L Hamilton
22   Becky Miles
23   Clyde Bunch

About The Authors

Lionel Ballard

Lionel is a Tampa and sports man from ground up. He attended George Washington Carver Elementary, Ernest E Just Jr. High School, graduated from Howard W. Blake High School in 1970. At Blake he was a member of the golf team and the 1969 Champion Football Team He attended Mississippi Valley State College. He retired from Tampa Electric Company after 40 years of service.

As for golf, its been a life long pursuit of the sound of "the ping" of a solid hit and long drive. Lionel has been an avid golfer since childhood and now serve on the Golf Advisory Board for the Tampa Sports Authority, as well as, being the Community Outreach Coordinator at First Tee Tampa Bay.

Lionel is passionate about the sport, the park and its history. Finding, and in some cases reconstructing, the elusive pieces of this book have been a labor of love for him.

Ersula K Odom

As CEO of Sula Too LLC, Ersula K. Odom is on a mission to preserve cultural history in any form possible. As such she is a publisher, legacy wall designer, legacy writer, and living history performer. She is also founder of Ersula's History Shop and the non-profit company Rescuing History, Inc. Collectively, all of her skills lead to preparing your story, rather average and ordinary or extraordinary, to take its rightful place in our history.

Ersula combines research, life and professional experiences of rural living, college life, fortune 500 corporate management, spirituality, family, entrepreneurship, sales, genealogy, and publishing, to deliver relative multi-generational and multi-cultural products and services.

Other books by Ersula K Odom: At Sula's Feet The Doris Ross Reddick Story Miss Lizzy's Story African Americans of Tampa Pamala McCoy-A Shero's Story Create Your Signature Book In A Weekend.